Cooking with Herbs: Adding Flavor and Health

Hseham Amrahs

Published by mds0, 2023.

COOKING WITH HERBS: ADDING FLAVOR AND HEALTH

First edition. April 30, 2023.

ISBN: 979-8223063179

Written by Hseham Amrahs.

Table of Contents

Preface

Cooking with herbs has been an essential part of culinary traditions for centuries. From basil in Italy to cilantro in Mexico, herbs have been used to add flavor, aroma, and health benefits to dishes around the world. Herbs not only make our meals taste better, but they also have numerous health benefits, making them a crucial ingredient in any dish.

This book, "Cooking with Herbs: Adding Flavor and Health," is a comprehensive guide to using herbs in your everyday cooking. Whether you are an experienced chef or a beginner in the kitchen, this book is designed to help you explore the world of herbs and learn how to use them to enhance the flavors of your dishes.

This book covers a wide range of herbs, from common herbs such as basil and thyme to more exotic herbs like lemongrass and tarragon. Each herb is presented with its history, flavor profile, and health benefits, giving you a better understanding of how to use it in your cooking. Additionally, this book includes tips on how to grow and store herbs, ensuring that you always have fresh herbs on hand for your meals.

The recipes in this book are designed to showcase the versatility of herbs and demonstrate how they can be used in a variety of dishes. From appetizers to desserts, there are recipes for every meal and occasion, including herb-infused cocktails, entrees, salads, and even ice cream. The recipes are easy to follow and include step-by-step instructions, making them accessible to anyone, regardless of their level of cooking experience.

Furthermore, this book emphasizes the health benefits of herbs, highlighting their antioxidant, anti-inflammatory, and antimicrobial properties. Using herbs in your cooking can be a simple and effective way to improve your overall health and wellbeing.

In conclusion, "Cooking with Herbs: Adding Flavor and Health" is a must-have guide for anyone looking to incorporate herbs into their cooking. With an extensive selection of herbs, easy-to-follow recipes, and emphasis on health benefits, this book is a valuable resource for anyone looking to elevate their culinary skills and improve their health. We hope that you find this book informative, inspiring, and enjoyable, and that it encourages you to explore the world of herbs and all the flavors and health benefits they have to offer.

—Author

1. Introduction to Cooking with Herbs

Herbs are an essential part of cooking, and they have been used for centuries to add flavor and aroma to meals. Not only do they enhance the taste of food, but they also have numerous health benefits. Whether you are a seasoned cook or a beginner, cooking with herbs is a great way to add variety and excitement to your dishes.

In this chapter, we will explore the basics of cooking with herbs, including how to select, store, and use herbs in your cooking. We will also discuss the health benefits of herbs and how to incorporate them into your diet for maximum health benefits.

Selecting Herbs

The first step in cooking with herbs is selecting the right ones for your dish. With so many different herbs available, it can be overwhelming to know which ones to choose. When selecting herbs, consider the flavors and aromas you want to add to your dish. Also, think about the type of dish you are making, as some herbs work better with certain foods than others.

Some common herbs to consider include:

Basil – This herb has a sweet, peppery flavor and is commonly used in Italian cuisine. It works well with tomatoes, mozzarella cheese, and pasta dishes.

Rosemary – This herb has a strong, earthy flavor and is commonly used in Mediterranean cuisine. It works well with roasted meats, potatoes, and bread.

Thyme – This herb has a subtle, lemony flavor and is commonly used in French cuisine. It works well with poultry, fish, and vegetables.

Sage – This herb has a strong, savory flavor and is commonly used in Italian and Mediterranean cuisine. It works well with poultry, pork, and pasta dishes.

Mint – This herb has a fresh, cool flavor and is commonly used in Middle Eastern and Mediterranean cuisine. It works well with lamb, yogurt, and salads.

Storing Herbs

Once you have selected your herbs, it is important to store them properly to ensure they stay fresh and flavorful. Herbs can be stored in several ways, depending on the type of herb and how long you plan to keep it.

Fresh herbs – Fresh herbs should be stored in the refrigerator in a plastic bag or container. Before storing, wash the herbs in cold water and dry them

thoroughly with a paper towel. To keep them fresh for longer, wrap them in a damp paper towel before placing them in the plastic bag or container.
Dried herbs – Dried herbs should be stored in a cool, dry place, such as a pantry or cabinet. They should be stored in airtight containers to prevent moisture from getting in.
Frozen herbs – Herbs can also be frozen to extend their shelf life. Wash the herbs and pat them dry, then chop or mince them and place them in ice cube trays. Add water or oil to cover the herbs, then freeze. Once frozen, transfer the herb cubes to a plastic bag and store them in the freezer.

Using Herbs

When using herbs in your cooking, it is important to use the right amount to achieve the desired flavor. Start by using a small amount and add more as needed. You can always add more, but it is difficult to remove excess herbs once they have been added.
To use fresh herbs, remove the leaves from the stem and chop them finely. For dried herbs, use about half the amount called for in a recipe, as they are more potent than fresh herbs. Add the herbs at the beginning of the cooking process to allow the flavors to develop and infuse into the dish.

Health Benefits of Herbs

In addition to adding flavor to your meals, herbs also have numerous health benefits. Many herbs contain antioxidants, which help protect your body from damage caused by free radicals. They also have anti-inflammatory properties, which can help reduce inflammation in the body and lower the risk of chronic diseases such as heart disease and cancer.
Some specific health benefits of common herbs include:
Basil – Basil contains antioxidants and anti-inflammatory compounds, as well as antimicrobial properties that can help fight bacteria and viruses.
Rosemary – Rosemary contains antioxidants and anti-inflammatory compounds that can help improve digestion and brain function. It may also have anti-cancer properties.
Thyme – Thyme contains antioxidants and anti-inflammatory compounds that can help improve respiratory health and boost the immune system.
Sage – Sage contains antioxidants and anti-inflammatory compounds that can help improve brain function and memory. It may also have antimicrobial properties that can help fight bacteria and viruses.

Mint – Mint contains antioxidants and anti-inflammatory compounds that can help improve digestion and relieve nausea. It may also have antimicrobial properties that can help fight bacteria and viruses.

Incorporating Herbs into Your Diet

There are many ways to incorporate herbs into your diet, from adding them to your cooking to using them in teas and other beverages. Here are a few ideas to get you started:

Add fresh herbs to salads for a burst of flavor and nutrition.

Use dried herbs to season meats, fish, and vegetables.

Make a homemade herb butter by mixing softened butter with finely chopped herbs.

Brew fresh or dried herbs in hot water for a soothing herbal tea.

Make a homemade herb vinaigrette by whisking together olive oil, vinegar, and finely chopped herbs.

In conclusion, cooking with herbs is a simple and delicious way to add flavor and nutrition to your meals. Whether you are a seasoned cook or a beginner, herbs can be used in a variety of dishes and cooking styles to enhance the taste and aroma of your food. With the right selection, storage, and use, herbs can become a staple in your kitchen and a valuable addition to your diet for their health benefits.

2. A Brief History of Herb Usage in Cooking

Herbs have been used in cooking for thousands of years, dating back to ancient times when they were not only valued for their culinary properties but also for their medicinal properties. The history of herb usage in cooking is a fascinating one that spans many cultures and time periods.

Ancient Times

Herb usage in cooking can be traced back to ancient times when they were used by the Egyptians, Greeks, and Romans. In fact, the Egyptians were known to have used herbs in their cooking as early as 2800 BC. They believed that herbs had medicinal properties that could be used to treat various ailments.

The Greeks and Romans also used herbs extensively in their cooking, often incorporating them into sauces and marinades. They also believed in the medicinal properties of herbs and used them to treat a wide range of illnesses.

Middle Ages

During the Middle Ages, herb usage in cooking continued to be popular, particularly in Europe. Herbs were used not only for their flavor but also for their medicinal properties, as they were believed to have healing powers.

During this time, many monasteries had gardens where herbs were grown for both culinary and medicinal purposes. The monks would use these herbs in their cooking and also create medicinal remedies using them.

Renaissance

The Renaissance period saw a renewed interest in the use of herbs in cooking, particularly in Italy. Italian chefs began to use herbs more extensively in their dishes, creating flavorful sauces and seasonings that are still popular today.

In fact, Italian cuisine is known for its use of herbs such as basil, oregano, and thyme, which are often used in dishes such as pasta sauces and pizza.

Modern Times

Herb usage in cooking has continued to evolve and expand in modern times, with many cultures around the world incorporating them into their cuisine. Today, herbs are used in a wide variety of dishes, from soups and stews to salads and sandwiches.

In addition to their culinary properties, herbs are also valued for their health benefits. Many herbs contain antioxidants and anti-inflammatory compounds that can help improve overall health and prevent chronic diseases.

In conclusion, the history of herb usage in cooking is a rich and varied one that spans many cultures and time periods. From the ancient Egyptians to modern-day chefs, herbs have been valued for their culinary and medicinal properties for thousands of years.

Today, herb usage in cooking continues to be popular, with many people recognizing the health benefits of incorporating them into their diet. Whether you are a seasoned cook or a beginner, herbs can be a valuable addition to your kitchen and a delicious way to add flavor and nutrition to your meals.

3. Understanding the Health Benefits of Herbs

Herbs have been used for their medicinal properties for centuries, and many modern studies have confirmed their health benefits. Incorporating herbs into your diet can be an easy and delicious way to improve your overall health and wellbeing. In this chapter, we will explore the many health benefits of herbs and how they can be used to promote a healthy lifestyle.

Antioxidant Properties

Many herbs contain antioxidants, which are compounds that help protect cells from damage caused by free radicals. Free radicals are molecules that can damage cells and contribute to the development of chronic diseases such as cancer, heart disease, and Alzheimer's disease.

Some of the most potent antioxidants found in herbs include flavonoids, phenolic acids, and carotenoids. These compounds help protect the body from oxidative stress and inflammation, which are both major contributors to chronic disease.

Anti-Inflammatory Properties

Inflammation is a natural process that helps the body fight off infections and heal injuries. However, chronic inflammation can lead to a host of health problems, including heart disease, diabetes, and arthritis.

Many herbs have anti-inflammatory properties that can help reduce inflammation in the body. For example, turmeric, ginger, and cinnamon have all been shown to have powerful anti-inflammatory effects.

Improved Digestion

Herbs have long been used to improve digestion and relieve digestive issues such as bloating, gas, and constipation. Many herbs contain compounds that help stimulate the digestive system and promote healthy gut bacteria.

For example, ginger has been shown to help relieve nausea and vomiting, while peppermint can help relieve symptoms of irritable bowel syndrome (IBS). Fennel is another herb that is commonly used to improve digestion and reduce bloating.

Boosted Immune System

Many herbs contain compounds that can help boost the immune system and prevent infections. For example, garlic contains allicin, a compound that has been shown to have antibacterial and antiviral properties.

Echinacea is another herb that is commonly used to boost the immune system and prevent colds and flu. Studies have shown that echinacea can help reduce the duration and severity of colds and flu symptoms.

Improved Brain Function

Herbs can also help improve brain function and reduce the risk of age-related cognitive decline. For example, rosemary has been shown to improve memory and concentration, while sage can help improve cognitive function in older adults.

Gingko biloba is another herb that is commonly used to improve brain function. It has been shown to improve cognitive function in people with Alzheimer's disease and may also improve memory in healthy individuals.

Reduced Stress and Anxiety

Herbs can also be used to help reduce stress and anxiety. Chamomile is a popular herb that is often used to promote relaxation and reduce anxiety.

Lavender is another herb that is commonly used to reduce stress and anxiety. Studies have shown that inhaling lavender essential oil can help reduce anxiety levels and improve sleep quality.

In conclusion, incorporating herbs into your diet is a simple and delicious way to improve your overall health and wellbeing. Herbs contain a wide variety of compounds that can help protect against chronic disease, improve digestion, boost the immune system, improve brain function, and reduce stress and anxiety.

Whether you are a seasoned cook or a beginner, there are many ways to incorporate herbs into your cooking, from adding them to salads and sauces to brewing them into teas and other beverages. With the right selection and use, herbs can become a valuable addition to your diet and a powerful tool for promoting a healthy lifestyle.

4. Choosing the Right Herbs for Your Dish

Choosing the right herbs for your dish can be a daunting task, especially if you are new to cooking with herbs. With so many different herbs available, each with its own unique flavor profile and culinary uses, it can be difficult to know where to start.

In this chapter, we will explore some tips and tricks for choosing the right herbs for your dish and how to pair them with different types of cuisine.

Consider the Flavor Profile

The first step in choosing the right herbs for your dish is to consider the flavor profile you are trying to achieve. Herbs can be categorized into several different flavor categories, including:

- Sweet: Herbs with a sweet flavor profile include basil, cinnamon, and mint.
- Spicy: Herbs with a spicy flavor profile include ginger, garlic, and cumin.
- Savory: Herbs with a savory flavor profile include thyme, rosemary, and sage.
- Bitter: Herbs with a bitter flavor profile include dandelion, chamomile, and turmeric.

Think about the flavor profile of the other ingredients in your dish and choose herbs that complement or balance those flavors. For example, if you are making a sweet dessert, you might want to choose herbs with a sweet or floral flavor, such as lavender or vanilla. If you are making a spicy dish, you might want to choose herbs with a spicy or pungent flavor, such as cilantro or chili flakes.

Consider the Cuisine

Another important factor to consider when choosing herbs for your dish is the type of cuisine you are preparing. Different cuisines often rely on specific herbs and spices to achieve their unique flavor profiles.

For example, Italian cuisine often uses basil, oregano, and thyme, while Indian cuisine often uses turmeric, cumin, and coriander. Mexican cuisine relies heavily on cilantro, while Thai cuisine uses a lot of lemongrass, galangal, and kaffir lime leaves.

Research the traditional herbs and spices used in the cuisine you are preparing and try to incorporate them into your dish. Not only will this help you achieve an authentic flavor, but it will also give you a deeper appreciation for the cultural significance of different herbs and spices.

Consider the Cooking Method

The cooking method you are using can also influence the herbs you choose for your dish. Some herbs are more robust and can stand up to high heat cooking methods, while others are more delicate and are best used raw or added at the end of cooking.

For example, rosemary and thyme are both robust herbs that can stand up to roasting and grilling, while basil and parsley are more delicate and are best used raw or added at the end of cooking.

Consider the Season

Many herbs are seasonal and may be more readily available and flavorful during certain times of the year. For example, basil is a summer herb and is best enjoyed during the warmer months, while sage and thyme are fall and winter herbs that pair well with hearty soups and stews.

Consider the Quantity

When it comes to cooking with herbs, a little goes a long way. Herbs are potent and can quickly overpower a dish if used in excess. It's important to use a light hand when adding herbs to your dishes and to taste as you go to ensure the flavor is balanced.

As a general rule, start with a small amount of herbs and gradually add more until you achieve the desired flavor. Remember that you can always add more herbs, but it's difficult to remove them once they have been added.

In conclusion, choosing the right herbs for your dish can take some practice, but with a little experimentation and research, you can quickly become a pro at pairing herbs with different types of cuisine and cooking methods.

When choosing herbs for your dish, consider the flavor profile you are trying to achieve, the cuisine you are preparing, the cooking method you are using, the season, and the quantity. By keeping these factors in mind, you can create flavorful and balanced dishes that showcase the unique flavors and benefits of different herbs.

Experimentation is key when it comes to cooking with herbs. Don't be afraid to try new combinations and see what works best for you. With a little bit of trial and error, you can create delicious dishes that are sure to impress.

5. Growing Your Own Herbs: A Beginner's Guide

Growing your own herbs is a great way to ensure a steady supply of fresh, flavorful herbs for your cooking needs. Not only is it cost-effective, but it also allows you to control the quality of the herbs you use in your dishes. In this chapter, we will provide a beginner's guide to growing your own herbs at home.

Choosing the Right Herbs

The first step in growing your own herbs is to choose the right herbs to grow. Consider the herbs you use most often in your cooking and select a few to get started with. Some easy-to-grow herbs for beginners include:

Basil, Chives, Mint, Oregano, Parsley, Rosemary, Sage, Thyme

These herbs are generally hardy and can thrive in a variety of growing conditions.

Selecting the Right Location

Herbs require a lot of sunlight to grow properly, so it's important to choose a location that receives at least 6-8 hours of direct sunlight each day. If you don't have a suitable outdoor space, you can grow herbs indoors on a windowsill or under artificial grow lights.

When choosing an outdoor location, consider factors such as soil quality, drainage, and exposure to the elements. Herbs prefer well-draining soil that is rich in organic matter, so it may be necessary to amend the soil with compost or other organic materials. It's also important to ensure proper drainage to prevent waterlogged soil, which can lead to root rot.

Preparing the Soil

Once you have selected a suitable location, it's time to prepare the soil for planting. Start by removing any weeds or debris from the area and loosening the soil with a garden fork or tiller. If your soil is poor quality, consider adding compost or other organic materials to improve the nutrient content.

Planting the Herbs

When planting herbs, it's important to give them enough space to grow and spread out. Generally, herbs should be spaced at least 12-18 inches apart to ensure proper airflow and prevent overcrowding.

When planting herbs, dig a hole that is slightly larger than the root ball and gently loosen the roots before placing the plant in the hole. Backfill the hole with soil and gently tamp it down around the base of the plant. Water the plant thoroughly after planting to help it settle in.

Caring for Your Herbs

Once your herbs are planted, it's important to care for them properly to ensure healthy growth and maximum flavor. Here are a few tips for caring for your herbs:

Water regularly: Herbs require regular watering to thrive, especially during hot, dry weather. Water the plants deeply at least once a week, and more often during hot, dry weather.

Fertilize sparingly: While herbs don't require a lot of fertilizer, they do benefit from occasional applications of organic fertilizers such as compost or fish emulsion. Apply fertilizers sparingly to avoid over-fertilizing.

Prune regularly: Regular pruning helps to promote bushier growth and prevents herbs from becoming too leggy. Use sharp, clean scissors or shears to remove 1/3 to 1/2 of the plant's growth at a time.

Harvest regularly: Regular harvesting not only ensures a steady supply of fresh herbs for your cooking needs but also helps to promote bushier growth. Avoid harvesting more than 1/3 of the plant's growth at a time to prevent damage.

Protect from pests: Herbs can be susceptible to pests such as aphids, mites, and whiteflies. Monitor your plants regularly for signs of infestation and treat promptly with organic pest control methods such as insecticidal soap or neem oil.

In conclusion, growing your own herbs is a rewarding and cost-effective way to ensure a steady supply of fresh, flavorful herbs for your cooking needs. With a little bit of planning and care, you can create a thriving herb garden that provides a variety of culinary benefits. Whether you have a large outdoor space or just a windowsill, there are plenty of herbs that can be grown successfully in a variety of growing conditions.

Remember to choose the right herbs for your needs, select a suitable growing location, prepare the soil properly, and care for your herbs regularly to ensure healthy growth and maximum flavor. With a little bit of time and effort, you can enjoy the benefits of fresh herbs in your cooking all year round.

6. The Art of Harvesting and Storing Herbs

Harvesting and storing herbs is an essential part of the herb-growing process. By knowing when and how to harvest your herbs, you can ensure that they are at their peak flavor and nutritional value when you use them in your cooking. Proper storage techniques can also help you to extend the lifespan of your herbs and prevent waste. In this chapter, we will discuss the art of harvesting and storing herbs to help you get the most out of your herb garden.

Harvesting Herbs

The best time to harvest herbs is when they are at their freshest and most flavorful. The ideal time for harvesting herbs is in the morning when the dew has dried, but before the sun gets too hot. This will help to ensure that the essential oils and flavors are at their peak.

When harvesting herbs, it is important to use sharp, clean scissors or pruning shears. Dull blades can crush the herbs, which can damage the plant and reduce the quality of the flavor. It is also important to only harvest healthy-looking leaves, as damaged or diseased leaves can spread infection to other parts of the plant.

There are two methods for harvesting herbs: the pinch and cut method and the stem cut method.

The pinch and cut method involves pinching off individual leaves or stems from the plant as needed. This method is ideal for herbs such as basil, parsley, and cilantro, which can be harvested continuously throughout the growing season.

The stem cut method involves cutting the entire stem of the herb plant just above a leaf node. This method is ideal for herbs such as rosemary, thyme, and sage, which can become woody and unproductive if not pruned regularly.

Storing Herbs

Proper storage is essential for maintaining the flavor and nutritional value of your herbs. There are several methods for storing herbs, including drying, freezing, and storing in oil or vinegar.

Drying Herbs

Drying herbs is a traditional method of preserving them for later use. To dry herbs, simply tie them into small bunches and hang them upside down in a warm, dry place with good air circulation. Once the herbs are dry and crumbly, strip the leaves from the stems and store them in an airtight container.

Freezing Herbs

Freezing herbs is another effective way to preserve their flavor and nutritional value. To freeze herbs, simply wash and chop them into small pieces, then place them in an ice cube tray and cover with water or oil. Once the cubes are frozen, transfer them to a freezer bag or container and store in the freezer until needed.

Storing in Oil or Vinegar

Storing herbs in oil or vinegar is another effective method for preserving their flavor. To store herbs in oil, simply fill a jar with fresh herbs and cover with olive oil. Store the jar in the refrigerator and use as needed. To store herbs in vinegar, simply fill a jar with fresh herbs and cover with vinegar. Store the jar in a cool, dark place and use as needed.

Tips for Storing Herbs

Regardless of the method you choose, there are several tips to keep in mind when storing herbs:

- Use airtight containers to prevent moisture and air from getting in.
- Label your containers with the name of the herb and the date it was stored.
- Store your herbs in a cool, dry place away from direct sunlight.
- Avoid storing herbs near strong-smelling foods, as they can absorb unwanted odors.
- Use your stored herbs within six months to ensure maximum flavor and nutritional value.

In conclusion, harvesting and storing herbs is an essential part of the herb-growing process. By knowing when and how to harvest your herbs and the different storage methods available, you can extend the lifespan of your herbs and ensure maximum flavor and nutritional value. Whether you choose to dry, freeze, or store your herbs in oil or vinegar, proper storage techniques can help you make the most of your herb garden and prevent waste. With a little practice, you can master the art of harvesting and storing herbs and enjoy fresh, flavorful herbs all year round.

7. Techniques for Preparing and Cooking with Herbs

Herbs are an essential ingredient in many dishes, and they can elevate the flavors of any meal. But how do you prepare and cook with herbs to maximize their flavor and health benefits? In this chapter, we'll explore some techniques for preparing and cooking with herbs.

Chopping Herbs

Chopping herbs is a simple way to release their flavor and aroma. To chop herbs, rinse them in cold water and pat them dry with a paper towel. Remove the leaves from the stems and discard the stems. Gather the leaves into a pile and chop them finely with a sharp knife. You can also use a food processor to chop herbs, but be careful not to over-process them, as this can turn them into a paste.

Bruising Herbs

Bruising herbs can also release their flavor and aroma. To bruise herbs, gently crush them with a mortar and pestle or the back of a knife. This technique works best for hardier herbs like rosemary and thyme.

Infusing Herbs

Infusing herbs is a great way to incorporate their flavor into liquids like oils, vinegars, and syrups. To infuse herbs, simply place them in a container with the liquid and let them steep for several hours or overnight. You can strain out the herbs before using the infused liquid.

Muddling Herbs

Muddling herbs is similar to bruising them, but it's usually done with softer herbs like mint and basil. To muddle herbs, place them in a glass with a small amount of liquid and gently crush them with a muddler or the back of a spoon. This technique is commonly used in cocktails and mocktails.

Pairing Herbs with Foods

Choosing the right herbs to pair with your food can make all the difference in the flavor of your dish. Here are some common pairings:

- Basil: pairs well with tomatoes, garlic, and olive oil.
- Rosemary: pairs well with chicken, potatoes, and lamb.
- Thyme: pairs well with roasted meats and vegetables.

- Sage: pairs well with pork and stuffing.
- Mint: pairs well with lamb, peas, and chocolate.

Cooking with Fresh vs. Dried Herbs

Fresh herbs have a stronger flavor than dried herbs, but dried herbs are more concentrated. If a recipe calls for fresh herbs but you only have dried herbs on hand, you can use half the amount of dried herbs. For example, if a recipe calls for 1 tablespoon of fresh rosemary, you can use 1/2 tablespoon of dried rosemary instead.

Adding Herbs to Your Cooking

When adding herbs to your cooking, it's best to add them towards the end of the cooking process. This helps preserve their flavor and aroma. For example, if you're making a pasta sauce with fresh basil, add the basil to the sauce a few minutes before it's done cooking.

Garnishing with Herbs

Garnishing with herbs is a great way to add a pop of color and flavor to your dish. Some common herbs used for garnishing include parsley, cilantro, and chives. To garnish with herbs, chop them finely and sprinkle them over your dish before serving.

Using Herb Blends

Herb blends are a convenient way to add flavor to your cooking without having to measure out multiple herbs. You can purchase pre-made herb blends or make your own by combining your favorite herbs. Common herb blends include Italian seasoning (basil, oregano, thyme), Herbes de Provence (rosemary, thyme, oregano), and curry powder (turmeric, cumin, coriander).

Experimenting with Herbs

Finally, don't be afraid to experiment with different herbs and flavor combinations in your cooking. Cooking with herbs is a creative process, and there's no right or wrong way to do it. Start by adding small amounts of herbs to your dishes and adjust the seasoning to taste. You may discover new flavor combinations that you love.

In addition to these techniques, there are a few things to keep in mind when preparing and cooking with herbs:

Always use fresh herbs whenever possible. They have a stronger flavor and aroma than dried herbs.

Wash your herbs thoroughly before using them to remove any dirt or debris.

Store fresh herbs in the refrigerator in a sealed container or plastic bag for up to a week. Dried herbs can be stored in a cool, dry place for up to a year.
Don't be afraid to use herbs in unconventional ways, like adding fresh mint to a fruit salad or using thyme in a marinade.
In conclusion, herbs are a versatile and delicious ingredient that can elevate the flavors of any dish. Whether you're chopping, bruising, infusing, or muddling, there are many techniques for preparing and cooking with herbs. By experimenting with different herbs and flavor combinations, you can take your cooking to the next level and create dishes that are both flavorful and healthy.

8. Incorporating Herbs into Breakfast and Brunch Dishes

When we think of cooking with herbs, we often think of savory dishes like soups, stews, and roasted meats. However, herbs can also be a great addition to breakfast and brunch dishes, adding a burst of flavor and freshness to your morning meal. Here are some tips and ideas for incorporating herbs into your breakfast and brunch dishes.

Omelets and Frittatas

Omelets and frittatas are a classic breakfast dish that can be easily customized with herbs. Start by whisking eggs together with a splash of milk and seasonings like salt and pepper. Then, add chopped fresh herbs like chives, parsley, and thyme to the egg mixture. Cook the eggs in a non-stick skillet over medium heat until they're set, then fold in your favorite fillings like cheese, cooked vegetables, or ham. Garnish with more fresh herbs for a pop of color and flavor.

Smoothie Bowls

Smoothie bowls are a trendy and healthy breakfast option that can be made even better with the addition of herbs. Start by blending frozen fruit, milk or yogurt, and a handful of leafy greens like spinach or kale in a blender. Then, add a handful of fresh herbs like mint, basil, or cilantro for a refreshing twist. Top with granola, nuts, and more fresh herbs for a colorful and flavorful breakfast bowl.

Pancakes and Waffles

Pancakes and waffles are a breakfast staple that can be made even more delicious with the addition of herbs. Add chopped fresh herbs like rosemary or thyme to your pancake or waffle batter for a savory twist. Serve with a dollop of herb-infused butter or a drizzle of maple syrup for a sweet and savory combination.

Breakfast Sandwiches

Breakfast sandwiches are a quick and easy breakfast option that can be made even better with the addition of herbs. Start by toasting an English muffin or bagel and adding a layer of cooked bacon or sausage. Then, add a fried egg and top with fresh herbs like chives, parsley, or basil. Serve with a side of fresh fruit or hash browns for a hearty and flavorful breakfast.

Breakfast Potatoes

Potatoes are a classic breakfast side dish that can be elevated with the addition of herbs. Start by cooking diced potatoes in a skillet with a little bit of oil until they're crispy and golden brown. Then, add chopped fresh herbs like rosemary, thyme, or sage for a savory twist. Serve alongside eggs and bacon for a classic breakfast spread.

Incorporating herbs into your breakfast and brunch dishes is a simple and delicious way to add flavor and freshness to your morning meal. Whether you're making omelets, smoothie bowls, pancakes, breakfast sandwiches, or potatoes, there's always a way to add a little bit of herbaceous goodness. Try experimenting with different herbs and flavor combinations to find your perfect breakfast or brunch recipe.

Breakfast Burritos

Breakfast burritos are a popular Tex-Mex dish that can be easily customized with herbs. Start by scrambling eggs in a skillet with diced peppers and onions. Then, add chopped fresh herbs like cilantro or parsley for a burst of freshness. Spoon the egg mixture onto a warm tortilla and top with shredded cheese, avocado, and salsa. Roll up the tortilla and enjoy a flavorful and filling breakfast.

Herb-Infused Butter

Herb-infused butter is a delicious and versatile ingredient that can be used to add flavor to any breakfast dish. Start by softening a stick of butter in a bowl. Then, finely chop fresh herbs like thyme, rosemary, or chives and mix them into the butter. Roll the butter into a log and chill in the refrigerator until firm. Slice the butter and use it to top pancakes, waffles, or toast for a savory twist.

Herb-Roasted Vegetables

Herb-roasted vegetables are a flavorful and healthy breakfast side dish that can be customized with your favorite herbs. Start by tossing chopped vegetables like potatoes, carrots, and bell peppers with olive oil, salt, and pepper. Then, add chopped fresh herbs like thyme, rosemary, or oregano and toss to coat. Roast the vegetables in the oven until they're tender and golden brown. Serve alongside eggs and toast for a hearty and delicious breakfast.

Herb-Infused Syrups

Herb-infused syrups are a sweet and flavorful way to add herbs to your breakfast dishes. Start by combining sugar and water in a saucepan and bringing it to a boil. Add chopped fresh herbs like basil, mint, or thyme and simmer for a few minutes until the flavors have infused. Strain the syrup through a fine-mesh sieve and use it to sweeten pancakes, waffles, or yogurt.

Herb-Infused Tea

Herb-infused tea is a simple and healthy way to incorporate herbs into your breakfast routine. Start by steeping fresh herbs like mint, chamomile, or lavender in hot water for a few minutes. Strain the tea and sweeten with honey or sugar if desired. Enjoy a warm and comforting cup of herb-infused tea alongside your breakfast for a soothing and flavorful start to your day.

Incorporating herbs into your breakfast and brunch dishes is a simple and delicious way to add flavor and health benefits to your morning meal. Whether you're making omelets, smoothie bowls, pancakes, breakfast sandwiches, or potatoes, there's always a way to add a little bit of herbaceous goodness. Try experimenting with different herbs and flavor combinations to find your perfect breakfast or brunch recipe.

9. Elevating Salads with Fresh Herbs

Salads are a great way to incorporate fresh vegetables and healthy ingredients into your diet. However, sometimes they can be bland or boring. Adding fresh herbs to your salads is an easy and delicious way to elevate their flavor and make them more exciting. In this chapter, we'll explore how to use fresh herbs to create delicious and flavorful salads.

Choosing the Right Herbs

When it comes to using fresh herbs in salads, there are many options to choose from. Some popular herbs for salads include basil, cilantro, parsley, dill, mint, and thyme. Each herb has its unique flavor profile and pairs well with different ingredients. For example, basil is a great complement to tomatoes and mozzarella, while cilantro works well with avocado and lime. Dill pairs nicely with cucumbers and yogurt dressing, while mint is great with berries and citrus.

It's important to choose fresh, high-quality herbs for your salads. Look for herbs that are bright in color, have a fresh scent, and are free from wilting or discoloration. You can either grow your herbs at home or purchase them at your local farmer's market or grocery store.

Washing and Preparing Herbs

Before using fresh herbs in your salads, it's important to wash and prepare them properly. Start by removing the leaves from the stems and discarding any wilted or discolored leaves. Rinse the leaves thoroughly under cold water to remove any dirt or debris. Gently pat the herbs dry with a paper towel or clean kitchen towel. It's important not to crush or bruise the herbs while washing, as this can damage their delicate flavor.

Once your herbs are washed and dried, you can prepare them for your salad. Depending on the herb, you may want to chop it finely, tear it into small pieces, or leave it whole. Consider the size and texture of the herb when deciding how to prepare it. For example, delicate herbs like cilantro and parsley can be chopped finely, while larger herbs like basil can be torn into small pieces.

Adding Herbs to Your Salad

There are many ways to incorporate fresh herbs into your salad. Here are a few ideas to get you started:

Toss fresh herbs with your greens: Instead of using plain lettuce or spinach, mix in a handful of chopped fresh herbs like parsley, mint, or cilantro. This will add a burst of fresh flavor to your salad and make it more interesting.
Use herbs as a garnish: Finely chop some herbs and sprinkle them over the top of your salad as a garnish. This will add a pop of color and flavor to your dish.
Make an herb dressing: Combine fresh herbs with olive oil, vinegar, and a pinch of salt to create a flavorful herb dressing. Use this dressing to dress your salad instead of a traditional vinaigrette.
Add herbs to your protein: If you're adding chicken, shrimp, or tofu to your salad, consider marinating it in a mixture of fresh herbs and olive oil before grilling or sautéing. This will infuse the protein with a delicious herbaceous flavor.
Use herbs as a base: Instead of using lettuce as the base of your salad, consider using fresh herbs like cilantro or basil. This will give your salad a unique flavor and texture.

Recipes

Here are a few salad recipes that incorporate fresh herbs:
Cucumber and Dill Salad: Combine sliced cucumbers, chopped fresh dill, and a simple vinaigrette for a refreshing and flavorful salad.
Caprese Salad with Basil: Layer sliced tomatoes, fresh mozzarella, and basil leaves on a plate. Drizzle with olive oil and balsamic vinegar for a classic and delicious salad.
Quinoa and adding olive oil, vinegar, salt, and pepper, but adding herbs can add depth and complexity to the flavor. For a basic herb vinaigrette, whisk together olive oil, red wine vinegar, dijon mustard, garlic, salt, and pepper, and then add in chopped fresh herbs such as parsley, basil, and chives.
For a creamy dressing, herbs can be blended with ingredients like Greek yogurt, sour cream, or mayonnaise to make a flavorful and satisfying dressing. A classic example is the creamy ranch dressing, which can be made by blending together mayonnaise, sour cream, buttermilk, garlic, onion powder, dill, parsley, and chives.

Herb Croutons

Croutons are a classic addition to salads, and herb croutons can add a delicious pop of flavor. To make herb croutons, start by cubing day-old bread, and then toss it with olive oil, salt, pepper, and chopped fresh herbs such as rosemary, thyme, and oregano. Bake in the oven until crispy and golden brown.

Herb Infused Oil

Herb infused oil can be used to add flavor to salads in a subtle yet effective way. Simply heat olive oil in a pan with fresh herbs such as thyme, rosemary, or basil until fragrant, and then remove from heat and let cool. Strain the oil to remove the herbs, and then use it to dress your salad or as a base for a homemade vinaigrette.

In conclusion, incorporating fresh herbs into salads can elevate their flavor and make them more exciting to eat. From herb dressings to herb croutons, there are many ways to use herbs to make salads more delicious and interesting. Don't be afraid to experiment with different herb combinations and techniques to find what works best for you. With a little creativity and some fresh herbs, you can take your salads to the next level.

10. Soups and Stews: The Perfect Vehicles for Herb Flavor

Soups and stews have been a staple in many cultures for centuries, and for good reason. They are warming, comforting, and nourishing, and they lend themselves well to the use of herbs for flavor and health benefits. In this chapter, we will explore the various ways in which herbs can be used to enhance the flavor of soups and stews, as well as their potential health benefits.

The Benefits of Using Herbs in Soups and Stews

Herbs have been used for thousands of years as both food and medicine. They are rich in phytonutrients, vitamins, and minerals that can help support overall health and wellbeing. When used in soups and stews, herbs can not only add flavor but also provide a range of health benefits. Here are a few examples:

Rosemary: Rosemary is a rich source of antioxidants and anti-inflammatory compounds, which can help reduce the risk of chronic diseases such as cancer and heart disease. It also has antimicrobial properties, which can help protect against foodborne illnesses.

Thyme: Thyme is another herb that is rich in antioxidants and has antimicrobial properties. It is also a good source of vitamin C, which can help boost the immune system.

Basil: Basil is a good source of vitamins A and K, as well as several essential minerals. It also contains compounds that have been shown to have anti-inflammatory and anti-cancer properties.

Parsley: Parsley is a good source of vitamin K, which is important for bone health. It also contains compounds that can help reduce inflammation and protect against oxidative stress.

Sage: Sage is a rich source of antioxidants and anti-inflammatory compounds, and it has been shown to have cognitive and memory-enhancing effects.

Using Fresh vs. Dried Herbs

When it comes to using herbs in soups and stews, you have the option of using either fresh or dried herbs. Both have their advantages and disadvantages, so it's up to you to decide which one to use based on your preferences and the recipe you're making.

Fresh herbs are generally more flavorful than dried herbs, and they also have a brighter color and aroma. However, they can be more expensive and may not be available year-round. Fresh herbs are best added towards the end of the cooking process to preserve their flavor and aroma.

Dried herbs, on the other hand, are more affordable and widely available, and they have a longer shelf life. They are also more concentrated than fresh herbs, so you need less of them to achieve the same flavor. However, they can be less flavorful than fresh herbs, and they can also lose their potency over time. Dried herbs are best added earlier in the cooking process to allow their flavors to develop.

How to Use Herbs in Soups and Stews

There are several ways to incorporate herbs into your soups and stews. Here are a few ideas:

Add herbs to the cooking liquid: One of the simplest ways to infuse your soup or stew with herb flavor is to add herbs directly to the cooking liquid. This will allow the flavors to meld together and create a rich, flavorful broth. Just be sure to remove any woody stems or tough leaves before adding the herbs to the pot.

Make a herb bundle or bouquet garni: Another way to infuse your soup or stew with herb flavor is to make a herb bundle or bouquet garni. This involves tying together a bundle of fresh herbs and adding it to the pot. The herbs can be easily removed at the end of cooking, so you don't have to worry about fishing out individual leaves or stems.

Use herb-infused oils: You can also add herb-infused oils to your soups and stews for an extra burst of flavor. Simply heat a neutral oil such as olive oil or grapeseed oil in a pan with your herbs until fragrant, then strain out the herbs and use the oil to sauté your vegetables or as a finishing drizzle over your finished soup or stew.

Add fresh herbs as a garnish: Adding fresh herbs as a garnish to your finished soup or stew can provide an extra pop of flavor and color. Chopped parsley, cilantro, or basil can be sprinkled over the top of your soup or stew just before serving.

Recipe Ideas

Here are a few recipe ideas that showcase the use of herbs in soups and stews:

Chicken Noodle Soup with Rosemary and Thyme

Ingredients:

- 1 pound boneless, skinless chicken breasts
- 1 onion, chopped
- 2 carrots, chopped
- 2 celery stalks, chopped
- 2 garlic cloves, minced
- 6 cups chicken broth
- 1 sprig rosemary
- 1 sprig thyme
- 8 ounces egg noodles
- Salt and pepper, to taste

Directions:

In a large pot, sauté the onion, carrots, and celery until soft.

Add the garlic and sauté for another minute.

Add the chicken broth, chicken breasts, rosemary, and thyme. Bring to a boil, then reduce heat and simmer for 20-30 minutes or until the chicken is cooked through.

Remove the chicken breasts and shred with two forks. Return the shredded chicken to the pot.

Add the egg noodles and simmer until cooked through, about 10 minutes.

Remove the rosemary and thyme sprigs and season with salt and pepper to taste.

Hearty Beef Stew with Parsley and Sage

Ingredients:

- 2 pounds beef stew meat
- 1 onion, chopped
- 2 carrots, chopped
- 2 celery stalks, chopped
- 2 garlic cloves, minced
- 4 cups beef broth
- 1 tablespoon tomato paste
- 1 tablespoon Worcestershire sauce
- 2 sprigs parsley
- 2 sprigs sage
- 2 bay leaves
- Salt and pepper, to taste

Directions:

In a large pot, brown the beef stew meat over medium-high heat until browned on all sides.

Add the onion, carrots, and celery and sauté until the vegetables are soft.

Add the garlic and sauté for another minute.

Add the beef broth, tomato paste, Worcestershire sauce, parsley, sage, and bay leaves. Bring to a boil, then reduce heat and simmer for 1-2 hours or until the beef is tender.

Remove the parsley, sage, and bay leaves and season with salt and pepper to taste.

Lentil Soup with Basil and Lemon

Ingredients:

- 1 onion, chopped
- 2 carrots, chopped
- 2 celery stalks, chopped
- 2 garlic cloves, minced
- 1 cup brown lentils
- 4 cups vegetable broth
- 1 sprig basil
- Juice of 1 lemon
- Salt and pepper, to taste

Directions:

In a large pot, sauté the onion, carrots, and celery until soft.

Add the garlic and sauté for another minute.

Add the lentils, vegetable broth, and basil. Bring to a boil, then reduce heat and simmer for 30-45 minutes or until the lentils are tender.

Remove the basil sprig and purée the soup with an immersion blender or in a blender until smooth.

5. Stir in the lemon juice and season with salt and pepper to taste.

In conclusion, soups and stews are the perfect vehicles for herb flavor, allowing for a range of herbs to be used to add depth and complexity to your dishes. Whether you prefer to use fresh or dried herbs, incorporating them into your soups and stews can elevate your meals and provide numerous health benefits. By experimenting with different herbs and techniques, you can create soups and stews that are both flavorful and nutritious. So next time you're making soup or stew, don't be afraid to add a little extra herb power. Your taste buds (and your body) will thank you!

11. Enhancing Appetizers and Snacks with Herb-infused Dips and Spreads

Appetizers and snacks are a staple of any party or gathering, but they don't have to be boring. By adding herb-infused dips and spreads to your repertoire, you can take your appetizers and snacks to the next level. Not only do these dips and spreads provide an extra burst of flavor, but they can also offer numerous health benefits. In this chapter, we'll explore how to enhance your appetizers and snacks with herb-infused dips and spreads.

Why Use Herb-Infused Dips and Spreads?

Herbs are a great way to add flavor to your dishes without relying on salt or fat. They are also packed with antioxidants and other health-promoting compounds. By using herbs in your dips and spreads, you can create flavorful and healthy options for your guests.

Additionally, dips and spreads are a versatile way to incorporate herbs into your diet. They can be served with a variety of different foods, including crackers, vegetables, and bread. Plus, they are easy to prepare and can be made ahead of time, making them a convenient option for entertaining.

Choosing Herbs for Dips and Spreads

When choosing herbs for your dips and spreads, it's important to consider the flavor profile you're trying to achieve. Some herbs have a stronger flavor than others, so you may need to adjust the amount you use depending on the recipe. Here are a few herbs that work well in dips and spreads:

Basil: Basil has a sweet and slightly peppery flavor that pairs well with tomatoes, cheese, and olive oil. It's a popular herb in Mediterranean cuisine and is often used in pesto.

Dill: Dill has a tangy and slightly bitter flavor that pairs well with fish, potatoes, and yogurt. It's a popular herb in Scandinavian cuisine and is often used in dips and sauces.

Rosemary: Rosemary has a strong and woody flavor that pairs well with meat, potatoes, and beans. It's a popular herb in Mediterranean cuisine and is often used in roasted dishes.

Thyme: Thyme has a slightly sweet and earthy flavor that pairs well with chicken, fish, and vegetables. It's a popular herb in French cuisine and is often used in soups and stews.
Parsley: Parsley has a mild and slightly bitter flavor that pairs well with garlic, lemon, and olive oil. It's a popular herb in Mediterranean cuisine and is often used as a garnish.

Herb-Infused Dip and Spread Ideas

Here are a few ideas for herb-infused dips and spreads to enhance your appetizers and snacks:

Garlic and Herb Dip

Ingredients:

- 1 cup plain Greek yogurt
- 2 garlic cloves, minced
- 2 tablespoons chopped fresh parsley
- 1 tablespoon chopped fresh dill
- 1 tablespoon chopped fresh chives
- Salt and pepper, to taste

Directions:

In a bowl, mix together the Greek yogurt, garlic, parsley, dill, and chives.
Season with salt and pepper to taste.
Serve with fresh vegetables, crackers, or pita chips.

Roasted Red Pepper and Basil Dip

Ingredients:

- 1 cup roasted red peppers, chopped
- 1/4 cup chopped fresh basil
- 1/4 cup grated Parmesan cheese
- 2 tablespoons olive oil
- 1 garlic clove, minced
- Salt and pepper, to taste

Directions:

In a blender or food processor, blend together the roasted red peppers, basil, Parmesan cheese, olive oil, and garlic until smooth.
Season with salt and pepper to taste.
Serve with crostini, crackers, or vegetables.

Feta and Herb

Ingredients:

- 4 ounces crumbled feta cheese
- 1/4 cup plain Greek yogurt
- 2 tablespoons chopped fresh parsley
- 2 tablespoons chopped fresh dill
- 1 garlic clove, minced
- 2 teaspoons lemon juice
- Salt and pepper, to taste

Directions:

In a bowl, mix together the feta cheese, Greek yogurt, parsley, dill, garlic, and lemon juice.

Season with salt and pepper to taste.

Serve with pita bread, crackers, or vegetables.

Avocado and Cilantro Dip

Ingredients:

- 2 ripe avocados, peeled and pitted
- 1/4 cup chopped fresh cilantro
- 1 jalapeño pepper, seeded and minced
- 2 tablespoons lime juice
- 1 garlic clove, minced
- Salt and pepper, to taste

Directions:

In a bowl, mash the avocados with a fork or a potato masher.

Mix in the cilantro, jalapeño pepper, lime juice, and garlic.

Season with salt and pepper to taste.

Serve with tortilla chips or vegetables.

Tips for Making Herb-Infused Dips and Spreads

Use fresh herbs whenever possible. They have a more vibrant flavor than dried herbs.

Don't be afraid to experiment with different herb combinations. You never know what delicious flavor you might come up with.

Adjust the amount of herbs you use based on your personal taste. If you prefer a stronger flavor, add more herbs. If you prefer a milder flavor, use less.

When making dips and spreads, consider the texture you want to achieve. If you want a smoother texture, use a blender or food processor. If you want a chunkier texture, use a fork or a potato masher.

In conclusion, herb-infused dips and spreads are an easy and delicious way to enhance your appetizers and snacks. By incorporating herbs into your dips and spreads, you can add flavor and nutrition to your dishes. With a little creativity and experimentation, you can create dips and spreads that are sure to impress your guests. So next time you're hosting a party or gathering, consider adding some herb-infused dips and spreads to your menu. Your taste buds (and your guests) will thank you!

12. Herb-marinated Meat and Poultry Recipes

Herbs have been used in cooking for centuries to add flavor, aroma, and nutritional value to dishes. One way to incorporate herbs into your cooking is by marinating meat and poultry. The process of marinating involves soaking meat in a mixture of herbs, spices, and other ingredients to infuse it with flavor and tenderness. In this chapter, we will explore some delicious herb-marinated meat and poultry recipes that are sure to impress your taste buds.

Rosemary and Garlic Grilled Lamb Chops

Ingredients:

- 8 lamb chops
- 1/4 cup olive oil
- 3 garlic cloves, minced
- 2 tablespoons chopped fresh rosemary
- Salt and pepper, to taste

Directions:

In a bowl, mix together the olive oil, garlic, and rosemary.

Season the lamb chops with salt and pepper.

Coat the lamb chops with the herb mixture.

Marinate in the refrigerator for at least 2 hours or overnight.

Preheat grill to medium-high heat.

Grill the lamb chops for about 3-4 minutes per side, or until cooked to your desired level of doneness.

Let the lamb chops rest for a few minutes before serving.

Lemon and Thyme Roasted Chicken

Ingredients:

- 1 whole chicken, cut into pieces
- 1/4 cup olive oil
- 3 garlic cloves, minced
- 2 tablespoons chopped fresh thyme
- 1 lemon, zested and juiced
- Salt and pepper, to taste

Directions:

Preheat oven to 400°F.

In a bowl, mix together the olive oil, garlic, thyme, lemon zest, and lemon juice.
Season the chicken pieces with salt and pepper.
Coat the chicken pieces with the herb mixture.
Marinate in the refrigerator for at least 2 hours or overnight.
Arrange the chicken pieces in a roasting pan.
Roast the chicken for about 35-40 minutes, or until cooked through and golden brown.
Let the chicken rest for a few minutes before serving.

Sage and Mustard Pork Tenderloin

Ingredients:

- 2 pork tenderloins
- 1/4 cup olive oil
- 3 garlic cloves, minced
- 2 tablespoons chopped fresh sage
- 2 tablespoons Dijon mustard
- Salt and pepper, to taste

Directions:

Preheat oven to 375°F.
In a bowl, mix together the olive oil, garlic, sage, and Dijon mustard.
Season the pork tenderloins with salt and pepper.
Coat the pork tenderloins with the herb mixture.
Marinate in the refrigerator for at least 2 hours or overnight.
Heat a large oven-safe skillet over medium-high heat.
Sear the pork tenderloins on all sides until browned.
Transfer the skillet to the oven and roast for about 15-20 minutes, or until cooked through.
Let the pork tenderloins rest for a few minutes before serving.

Tips for Marinating Meat and Poultry with Herbs

Choose the right herbs. Some herbs work better with certain meats than others. For example, rosemary pairs well with lamb, thyme with chicken, and sage with pork.
Use fresh herbs whenever possible. They have a more vibrant flavor than dried herbs.
Don't over-marinate. Marinating meat for too long can result in a mushy texture. Aim for no more than 24 hours in the refrigerator.

Use a non-reactive container. Avoid using metal or plastic containers for marinating meat as they can react with acidic ingredients and affect the taste of the dish. Glass or ceramic containers are a better choice.

Use enough marinade. Make sure the meat is completely coated in the marinade so that it can absorb as much flavor as possible.

Keep it chilled. Always marinate meat in the refrigerator, not at room temperature, to prevent bacteria growth.

Pat dry before cooking. Before cooking, remove the meat from the marinade and pat it dry with paper towels. This helps to ensure a crispy exterior and even cooking.

In conclusion, herb-marinated meat and poultry recipes are a great way to add flavor and nutritional value to your dishes. The combination of herbs, spices, and other ingredients in the marinade not only enhances the taste of the meat but also helps to tenderize it. The recipes mentioned above are just a few examples of the many ways you can incorporate herbs into your cooking. So, don't be afraid to experiment and try out new herb combinations to create delicious and healthy meals for you and your loved ones.

13. Herb-rubbed Roasts and Steaks

Roasts and steaks are a classic staple in many cuisines, and for good reason - they are versatile, easy to cook, and delicious. But if you're looking to add some variety and depth of flavor to your roasts and steaks, consider using herb rubs. Herb rubs are a simple yet effective way to add complexity and nuance to your meat dishes, and can be made with a wide variety of herbs and spices. In this chapter, we'll explore the art of herb-rubbed roasts and steaks, and offer some tips and recipes to get you started.

Choosing Herbs and Spices for Your Rub

When it comes to choosing herbs and spices for your rub, the possibilities are nearly endless. Here are some popular choices to consider:

Rosemary: A classic choice for herb-rubbed meat, rosemary has a woody, piney flavor that pairs well with beef and lamb.

Thyme: Another popular choice, thyme has a slightly sweet and earthy flavor that complements a wide range of meats.

Sage: With its slightly bitter and savory flavor, sage is a great choice for pork and chicken dishes.

Garlic: While not technically an herb, garlic is a popular ingredient in many herb rubs. Its pungent, spicy flavor pairs well with nearly any type of meat.

Black pepper: A staple spice in many kitchens, black pepper adds a subtle heat and depth of flavor to your rub.

Paprika: This vibrant red spice has a smoky, slightly sweet flavor that pairs well with beef and pork.

Cumin: Often used in Middle Eastern and Latin American cuisine, cumin has a warm, earthy flavor that complements beef and lamb.

Creating Your Rub

To create your herb rub, start by selecting your herbs and spices of choice. Measure out the ingredients and mix them together in a small bowl. If you have a mortar and pestle, you can grind the herbs and spices together to create a more cohesive rub. Be sure to crush any whole spices, such as peppercorns or cumin seeds, before adding them to the mix.

Once you've created your rub, it's time to apply it to your meat. First, pat the meat dry with paper towels to remove any excess moisture. Then, apply the rub generously to all sides of the meat, pressing it into the surface to ensure it adheres well.

Cooking Your Herb-Rubbed Meat

Now that you've applied your herb rub, it's time to cook your meat. Here are some tips for ensuring a perfectly cooked herb-rubbed roast or steak:

Let it come to room temperature. Before cooking, allow your meat to sit at room temperature for at least 30 minutes. This helps to ensure even cooking and a tender, juicy result.

Use high heat. Whether you're roasting or grilling your meat, it's important to use high heat to create a crispy exterior and seal in the juices. For roasts, start with a high heat for the first 15-20 minutes, then lower the temperature to finish cooking. For steaks, sear them over high heat for a few minutes on each side before finishing them in the oven.

Use a meat thermometer. The best way to ensure your meat is cooked to your desired level of doneness is to use a meat thermometer. For steaks, aim for an internal temperature of 125°F for medium-rare, 135°F for medium, and 145°F for medium-well. For roasts, aim for 135°F for medium-rare and 145°F for medium.

Let it rest. After cooking, let your meat rest for at least 10-15 minutes before slicing or serving. This allows the juices to redistribute throughout the meat, resulting in a more tender and flavorful dish.

Herb-Rubbed Roast Recipe

Here's a simple yet flavorful herb-rubbed roast recipe to try:

Ingredients:

- 3 lb beef roast (such as ribeye or sirloin)
- 2 tbsp chopped fresh rosemary
- 2 tbsp chopped fresh thyme
- 1 tbsp minced garlic
- 1 tbsp black pepper
- 1 tsp salt
- 2 tbsp olive oil

Directions:

Preheat your oven to 450°F.

In a small bowl, mix together the rosemary, thyme, garlic, black pepper, salt, and olive oil to create your herb rub.

Pat the beef roast dry with paper towels, then apply the herb rub generously to all sides of the meat.
Place the roast on a rack in a roasting pan and cook in the preheated oven for 15 minutes.
Reduce the oven temperature to 325°F and continue cooking until the internal temperature of the roast reaches 135°F for medium-rare, about 1-1.5 hours.
Remove the roast from the oven and let it rest for 10-15 minutes before slicing and serving.
In conclusion, herb-rubbed roasts and steaks are a delicious and easy way to elevate your meat dishes. With a wide range of herbs and spices to choose from, you can customize your rub to suit your taste preferences and the type of meat you're cooking. Remember to let your meat come to room temperature, use high heat, and use a meat thermometer to ensure perfect results every time. Give herb-rubbed roasts and steaks a try, and enjoy the added depth of flavor and health benefits that herbs bring to your dishes.

14. Herb-enhanced Seafood Dishes

Seafood is a delicious and healthy protein source that can be enhanced with the use of herbs. Herbs can add depth and complexity to seafood dishes, bringing out their natural flavors and aromas. In this chapter, we'll explore different herbs and how they can be used to enhance seafood dishes.

Benefits of Adding Herbs to Seafood

Herbs are not only a great way to add flavor to seafood, but they also have numerous health benefits. Many herbs have anti-inflammatory properties and are packed with antioxidants, vitamins, and minerals that can support a healthy immune system. Adding herbs to your seafood dishes can also help to reduce the amount of salt and fat needed to achieve a delicious flavor.

Popular Herbs for Seafood

Dill - Dill is a delicate herb with a subtle anise flavor that pairs well with fish and seafood. It's commonly used in Nordic and Eastern European cuisines and is often paired with salmon, shrimp, and crab.

Tarragon - Tarragon has a sweet, anise-like flavor with a hint of vanilla. It's commonly used in French cuisine and pairs well with white fish and shellfish like scallops and shrimp.

Thyme - Thyme has a savory flavor with a slight lemony aroma. It pairs well with grilled or roasted seafood and can be used in marinades and herb rubs.

Basil - Basil has a sweet and slightly peppery flavor that pairs well with seafood like shrimp, scallops, and white fish. It's commonly used in Italian and Southeast Asian cuisine.

Parsley - Parsley has a fresh, grassy flavor that pairs well with white fish and shellfish like mussels and clams. It's often used as a garnish for seafood dishes.

Herb-Enhanced Seafood Recipes

Lemon Herb Grilled Shrimp

Ingredients:

- 1 lb large shrimp, peeled and deveined
- 2 tbsp chopped fresh parsley
- 1 tbsp chopped fresh thyme
- 1 tbsp chopped fresh oregano
- 2 garlic cloves, minced

- 1/4 cup olive oil
- Juice of 1 lemon
- Salt and pepper to taste

Directions:

In a large bowl, mix together the parsley, thyme, oregano, garlic, olive oil, lemon juice, salt, and pepper.

Add the shrimp to the bowl and toss to coat in the herb mixture.

Preheat your grill to medium-high heat.

Thread the shrimp onto skewers and grill for 2-3 minutes per side, until pink and slightly charred.

Serve hot with lemon wedges.

Baked Salmon with Herb Crust

Ingredients:

- 4 salmon fillets
- 1/4 cup chopped fresh parsley
- 1/4 cup chopped fresh dill
- 1/4 cup chopped fresh thyme
- 2 garlic cloves, minced
- 1/4 cup panko breadcrumbs
- 1/4 cup grated parmesan cheese
- 2 tbsp olive oil
- Salt and pepper to taste

Directions:

Preheat your oven to 400°F.

In a small bowl, mix together the parsley, dill, thyme, garlic, panko breadcrumbs, parmesan cheese, olive oil, salt, and pepper.

Place the salmon fillets on a baking sheet lined with parchment paper.

Spread the herb mixture evenly over the top of each salmon fillet.

Bake in the preheated oven for 10-12 minutes, or until the salmon is cooked through and the crust is golden brown.

Serve hot with lemon wedges.

In conclusion, adding herbs to your seafood dishes is a simple and delicious way to elevate their flavors and add nutritional benefits. Whether you prefer delicate herbs like dill and tarragon or savory herbs like thyme and rosemary, there are many ways to incorporate herbs into your seafood dishes.

Herbs can be used in marinades, herb rubs, dips, and sauces to add depth and complexity to your seafood dishes. They can also be used as a garnish to add a fresh, herbaceous flavor to your finished dish. Remember, herbs not only add flavor to your dishes but also have numerous health benefits. By adding herbs to your seafood dishes, you can create delicious and healthy meals that everyone will enjoy.

15. Vegetarian and Vegan Herb-centric Recipes

As the popularity of vegetarian and vegan diets continues to grow, people are discovering the joys of cooking with herbs to add flavor and nutrition to plant-based dishes. Herbs are an excellent way to elevate the flavors of vegetables and grains and can be used in a variety of ways, from simple herb garnishes to more complex herb-infused sauces and dressings.

In this chapter, we will explore some popular herbs for vegetarian and vegan cooking and share two delicious recipes: Herb and Mushroom Quinoa Pilaf and Roasted Vegetable Salad with Herb Dressing. These recipes are a great starting point for experimenting with herbs in your vegetarian and vegan dishes, but don't be afraid to get creative and try new combinations.

Popular Herbs for Vegetarian and Vegan Cooking

Basil: A versatile herb that adds a sweet, slightly peppery flavor to dishes. Basil pairs well with tomatoes, eggplant, zucchini, and other summer vegetables.

Cilantro: Also known as coriander, cilantro adds a fresh, citrusy flavor to dishes. It is commonly used in Mexican and Asian cuisine and pairs well with beans, rice, and grilled vegetables.

Dill: A delicate herb with a subtle anise flavor, dill is commonly used in Scandinavian and Eastern European cuisine. It pairs well with potatoes, carrots, beets, and cucumbers.

Oregano: A pungent herb with a slightly bitter, lemony flavor, oregano is commonly used in Mediterranean cuisine. It pairs well with tomatoes, eggplant, and pasta dishes.

Rosemary: A fragrant herb with a piney, slightly bitter flavor, rosemary is commonly used in Italian and Mediterranean cuisine. It pairs well with roasted vegetables, potatoes, and beans.

Sage: A pungent herb with a slightly bitter, earthy flavor, sage is commonly used in Italian and Mediterranean cuisine. It pairs well with mushrooms, roasted vegetables, and beans.

Herb and Mushroom Quinoa Pilaf

Ingredients:

- 1 cup quinoa, rinsed and drained
- 2 cups vegetable broth

- 1 tablespoon olive oil
- 1 onion, chopped
- 2 cloves garlic, minced
- 1 cup sliced mushrooms
- 1 tablespoon chopped fresh thyme
- 1 tablespoon chopped fresh rosemary
- Salt and pepper, to taste

Instructions:

In a medium saucepan, combine the quinoa and vegetable broth. Bring to a boil, then reduce heat to low and simmer for 15-20 minutes, or until the quinoa is tender and the liquid is absorbed.

While the quinoa is cooking, heat the olive oil in a large skillet over medium heat. Add the onion and garlic and cook for 2-3 minutes, or until the onion is soft and translucent.

Add the mushrooms to the skillet and cook for 5-7 minutes, or until they are tender and lightly browned.

Stir in the fresh thyme and rosemary and cook for an additional 1-2 minutes, or until fragrant.

Stir the herb and mushroom mixture into the cooked quinoa. Season with salt and pepper, to taste.

Roasted Vegetable Salad with Herb Dressing

Ingredients:

For the salad:

- 2 cups chopped mixed vegetables (such as bell peppers, zucchini, eggplant, and cherry tomatoes)
- 2 cloves garlic, minced
- 2 tablespoons olive oil
- Salt and pepper, to taste
- For the herb dressing:
- 1/2 cup chopped fresh basil
- 1/2 cup chopped fresh parsley
- 2 tablespoons chopped fresh chives
- 2 cloves garlic, minced
- 1/4 cup olive oil
- 2 tablespoons red wine vinegar

- Salt and pepper, to taste

Instructions:

Preheat the oven to 400°F (200°C). Line a baking sheet with parchment paper.
In a bowl, combine the chopped vegetables, garlic, olive oil, salt, and pepper. Toss to coat.
Spread the vegetables in a single layer on the prepared baking sheet. Roast for 20-25 minutes, or until tender and lightly browned.
While the vegetables are roasting, make the herb dressing. In a small bowl, whisk together the chopped basil, parsley, chives, garlic, olive oil, red wine vinegar, salt, and pepper.
When the vegetables are done, transfer them to a large bowl. Drizzle the herb dressing over the top and toss to coat.
Serve the salad warm or at room temperature.
In conclusion, herbs are a fantastic addition to vegetarian and vegan dishes, adding flavor, nutrition, and a touch of elegance. From simple herb garnishes to more complex herb-infused sauces and dressings, there are countless ways to incorporate herbs into your plant-based dishes. Experiment with different herbs and flavor combinations to find the perfect match for your taste buds. Whether you are a vegetarian or a vegan, herbs are an excellent way to add variety and excitement to your meals.

16. Classic Italian Dishes with Fresh Herbs

When it comes to classic Italian dishes, fresh herbs play a crucial role in elevating the flavors to a whole new level. Italian cuisine is known for its simplicity and use of fresh, seasonal ingredients, and herbs are no exception. From basil to oregano, rosemary to thyme, Italian cooking incorporates a variety of herbs in various dishes. In this chapter, we will explore some classic Italian dishes with fresh herbs that are easy to prepare and will undoubtedly impress your taste buds.

Pesto alla Genovese

Pesto alla Genovese is a classic Italian sauce originating from the Liguria region of Italy. This sauce is traditionally made with fresh basil, garlic, pine nuts, Parmesan cheese, and extra virgin olive oil. The key to making a great pesto is to use fresh ingredients and a mortar and pestle to blend the herbs and nuts. However, you can also use a food processor or blender to make the pesto.

Ingredients:

- 2 cups fresh basil leaves, packed
- 1/2 cup freshly grated Parmesan cheese
- 1/2 cup extra-virgin olive oil
- 1/3 cup pine nuts
- 3 garlic cloves, peeled
- Salt and freshly ground black pepper, to taste

Instructions:

In a food processor or blender, pulse the basil, garlic, and pine nuts until coarsely chopped.

Add the Parmesan cheese and pulse again until well combined.

With the food processor or blender running, slowly pour in the olive oil until the pesto is smooth and well combined.

Season with salt and pepper to taste.

Pesto alla Genovese can be used in a variety of ways. It is commonly used as a sauce for pasta dishes, as a spread for sandwiches or crostini, or as a dip for vegetables.

Insalata Caprese

Insalata Caprese, also known as Caprese salad, is a classic Italian salad originating from the island of Capri. This salad is made with fresh tomatoes, mozzarella cheese, and basil, drizzled with extra-virgin olive oil and balsamic vinegar. This salad is perfect for summertime and pairs well with grilled meats or fish.

Ingredients:

- 4 large ripe tomatoes, sliced
- 1 pound fresh mozzarella cheese, sliced
- 1/2 cup fresh basil leaves, chopped
- 1/4 cup extra-virgin olive oil
- 2 tablespoons balsamic vinegar
- Salt and freshly ground black pepper, to taste

Instructions:

Arrange the sliced tomatoes and mozzarella cheese on a platter.

Sprinkle the chopped basil over the top.

Drizzle with the olive oil and balsamic vinegar.

Season with salt and pepper to taste.

Insalata Caprese is a simple and delicious dish that is perfect for any occasion.

Bruschetta al Pomodoro

Bruschetta al Pomodoro is a classic Italian appetizer that is made with toasted bread, fresh tomatoes, garlic, basil, and extra-virgin olive oil. This dish is perfect for entertaining and is always a crowd-pleaser.

Ingredients:

- 6-8 slices of crusty bread
- 4 ripe tomatoes, diced
- 2 garlic cloves, minced
- 1/4 cup fresh basil leaves, chopped
- 1/4 cup extra-virgin olive oil
- Salt and freshly ground black pepper, to taste

Instructions:

Preheat the oven to 400°F.

Arrange the bread slices on a baking sheet and brush with olive oil.

Toast in the oven for 8-10 minutes or until golden brown.

In a bowl, combine the diced tomatoes, minced garlic, chopped basil, and extra-virgin olive oil.

5. Season with salt and pepper to taste.
Spoon the tomato mixture onto the toasted bread slices.
Serve immediately.
Bruschetta al Pomodoro is a perfect appetizer to serve before a pasta dinner, or as a light lunch.

Spaghetti Aglio e Olio

Spaghetti Aglio e Olio is a classic Italian pasta dish that is made with spaghetti, garlic, red pepper flakes, and parsley. This dish is simple yet flavorful and is perfect for a quick and easy weeknight meal.

Ingredients:

- 1 pound spaghetti
- 1/2 cup extra-virgin olive oil
- 6 garlic cloves, thinly sliced
- 1/2 teaspoon red pepper flakes
- 1/2 cup fresh parsley leaves, chopped
- Salt and freshly ground black pepper, to taste

Instructions:

Cook the spaghetti according to package instructions until al dente.
While the spaghetti is cooking, heat the olive oil in a large skillet over medium heat.
Add the garlic and red pepper flakes and cook until fragrant, about 1-2 minutes.
Reserve 1 cup of the pasta cooking water, then drain the spaghetti and add it to the skillet.
Toss the spaghetti with the garlic and oil until well coated.
Add the reserved pasta water, a little at a time, until the spaghetti is well coated and the sauce is creamy.
Add the chopped parsley and toss to combine.
Season with salt and pepper to taste.
Spaghetti Aglio e Olio is a simple and delicious pasta dish that can be made in under 30 minutes.

Osso Buco

Osso Buco is a classic Italian dish that originated in Milan. This dish is made with veal shanks that are braised in a flavorful tomato-based sauce with vegetables, herbs, and white wine. This dish is perfect for a special occasion or when you want to impress your guests.

Ingredients:

- 4 veal shanks, about 1 1/2 inches thick
- Salt and freshly ground black pepper, to taste
- 1/2 cup all-purpose flour
- 1/4 cup extra-virgin olive oil
- 1 onion, chopped
- 2 carrots, chopped
- 2 celery stalks, chopped
- 4 garlic cloves, minced
- 1 tablespoon tomato paste
- 1/2 cup white wine
- 1 can (28 oz) crushed tomatoes
- 2 cups beef broth
- 2 bay leaves
- 2 sprigs fresh thyme
- 1/4 cup fresh parsley leaves, chopped
- 1 tablespoon lemon zest

Instructions:

Season the veal shanks with salt and pepper, then dredge in the flour, shaking off any excess.

Heat the olive oil in a large Dutch oven over medium-high heat.

Add the veal shanks and brown on both sides, about 5 minutes per side.

Remove the veal shanks and set aside.

Add the onion, carrots, celery, and garlic to the Dutch oven and cook until softened, about 5 minutes.

Stir in the tomato paste and cook for 1-2 minutes.

Add the white wine and bring to a simmer.

Add the crushed tomatoes, beef broth, bay leaves, and thyme.

Return the veal shanks to the Dutch oven and spoon the sauce over them.

Cover and simmer over low heat for 2-3 hours, or until the meat is tender and falls off the bone.

Discard the bay leaves and thyme sprigs.

Stir in the chopped parsley and lemon zest.

Season with salt and pepper to taste.
Serve the Osso Buco hot, with crusty bread to soak up the delicious sauce.
Osso Buco is a classic Italian dish that is perfect for a special occasion or a hearty family dinner. The veal shanks are braised in a flavorful tomato-based sauce with vegetables, herbs, and white wine, resulting in a tender and flavorful dish.

Pesto

Pesto is a classic Italian sauce that is made with fresh basil, pine nuts, garlic, Parmesan cheese, and olive oil. This sauce is versatile and can be used as a topping for pasta, pizza, bread, and more.

Ingredients:

- 2 cups fresh basil leaves, packed
- 1/2 cup pine nuts
- 2 garlic cloves, minced
- 1/2 cup grated Parmesan cheese
- 1/2 cup extra-virgin olive oil
- Salt and freshly ground black pepper, to taste

Instructions:

In a food processor, pulse the basil, pine nuts, and garlic until coarsely chopped.
Add the Parmesan cheese and pulse until well combined.
With the motor running, slowly pour in the olive oil until the pesto is smooth and creamy.
Season with salt and pepper to taste.
Pesto is a versatile sauce that can be used as a topping for pasta, pizza, bread, and more. It is easy to make and can be stored in the refrigerator for up to a week.
In conclusion, classic Italian dishes with fresh herbs are a great way to add flavor and health to your meals. From appetizers like Bruschetta al Pomodoro to main dishes like Osso Buco, these dishes are easy to make and delicious to eat. Fresh herbs like basil, parsley, and thyme add a burst of flavor to these dishes, and they also provide health benefits like anti-inflammatory properties and antioxidants. So why not add some fresh herbs to your next Italian meal and enjoy the delicious flavors and health benefits they provide?

17. French-inspired Recipes Featuring Herbs

French cuisine is known for its rich flavors and elegant presentation, and herbs play a crucial role in achieving these qualities. French chefs use a variety of herbs to add depth and complexity to their dishes, from the robust thyme and rosemary to the delicate tarragon and chervil. In this chapter, we will explore some classic French-inspired recipes that feature herbs and learn how to incorporate these flavors into our own cooking.

Herb-Crusted Salmon

Ingredients:

- 4 salmon fillets, skin-on
- 1/4 cup chopped fresh parsley
- 1/4 cup chopped fresh thyme
- 1/4 cup chopped fresh chives
- 1/4 cup chopped fresh dill
- 1/4 cup panko bread crumbs
- 2 tablespoons Dijon mustard
- 2 tablespoons olive oil
- Salt and freshly ground black pepper

Instructions:

Preheat the oven to 400°F.

In a small bowl, combine the parsley, thyme, chives, dill, and panko bread crumbs.

Season the salmon fillets with salt and pepper.

Brush the top of each fillet with Dijon mustard.

Divide the herb and bread crumb mixture evenly among the fillets, pressing it onto the mustard-coated tops.

Heat the olive oil in an oven-safe skillet over medium-high heat.

Add the salmon fillets to the skillet, skin-side down, and cook for 2-3 minutes until the skin is crispy.

Transfer the skillet to the oven and bake for 8-10 minutes, or until the salmon is cooked through.

This herb-crusted salmon recipe is a delicious and healthy way to incorporate herbs into your meals. The combination of parsley, thyme, chives, and dill provides a burst of fresh flavor that pairs perfectly with the rich and buttery salmon. Plus, the panko bread crumbs add a satisfying crunch to every bite.

Roasted Chicken with Herbs de Provence

Ingredients:

- 1 whole chicken, about 4 pounds
- 2 tablespoons Herbs de Provence
- 1 lemon, sliced
- 3 cloves garlic, minced
- 2 tablespoons olive oil
- Salt and freshly ground black pepper

Instructions:

Preheat the oven to 425°F.

Rinse the chicken and pat dry with paper towels.

In a small bowl, mix together the Herbs de Provence, garlic, olive oil, salt, and pepper.

Rub the herb mixture all over the chicken, including the cavity.

Stuff the lemon slices into the chicken cavity.

Place the chicken in a roasting pan, breast-side up.

Roast for 1 hour and 15 minutes, or until the juices run clear when the chicken is pierced with a knife.

Let the chicken rest for 10 minutes before carving and serving.

Herbs de Provence is a classic French herb blend that typically includes thyme, rosemary, oregano, marjoram, and lavender. It adds a fragrant and earthy flavor to dishes, and pairs well with chicken, fish, and vegetables. This roasted chicken recipe showcases the flavor of Herbs de Provence, along with the brightness of lemon and the richness of garlic.

Mushroom and Herb Quiche

Ingredients:

- 1 pie crust, store-bought or homemade
- 4 tablespoons butter
- 1 onion, diced
- 2 cloves garlic, minced
- 8 ounces mushrooms, sliced
- 1/4 cup chopped fresh parsley
- 1/4 cup chopped fresh thyme

- 1/4 cup chopped fresh chives
- 4 eggs
- 1 cup milk
- 1/2 teaspoon salt
- Freshly ground black pepper

Instructions:

Preheat the oven to 375°F.

Place the pie crust in a 9-inch pie dish and crimp the edges.

In a large skillet, melt the butter over medium heat.

Add the onion and garlic and cook until softened, about 5 minutes.

Add the mushrooms and cook until they release their moisture and start to brown, about 10 minutes.

Stir in the parsley, thyme, and chives and remove from heat.

In a medium bowl, whisk together the eggs, milk, salt, and pepper.

Spoon the mushroom mixture into the pie crust.

Pour the egg mixture over the mushrooms.

Bake for 35-40 minutes, or until the quiche is set and the top is golden brown.

Quiche is a classic French dish that can be served for breakfast, lunch, or dinner. This mushroom and herb quiche is packed with flavor and nutrients from the fresh herbs and mushrooms. The combination of parsley, thyme, and chives gives the quiche a bright and herbaceous flavor that complements the earthy and savory mushrooms.

Herb and Goat Cheese Stuffed Chicken Breasts

Ingredients:

- 4 boneless, skinless chicken breasts
- 4 ounces goat cheese
- 1/4 cup chopped fresh basil
- 1/4 cup chopped fresh parsley
- 1/4 cup chopped fresh chives
- 2 cloves garlic, minced
- Salt and freshly ground black pepper
- 2 tablespoons olive oil

Instructions:

Preheat the oven to 375°F.

In a small bowl, mix together the goat cheese, basil, parsley, chives, and garlic.

Season the chicken breasts with salt and pepper.
Cut a slit into the side of each chicken breast, creating a pocket for the filling.
Stuff each chicken breast with 1/4 of the herb and goat cheese mixture.
Heat the olive oil in an oven-safe skillet over medium-high heat.
Add the chicken breasts to the skillet and cook for 3-4 minutes on each side, until browned.
Transfer the skillet to the oven and bake for 15-20 minutes, or until the chicken is cooked through.
This herb and goat cheese stuffed chicken recipe is a great way to add flavor and richness to your chicken dishes. The combination of basil, parsley, and chives gives the goat cheese filling a fresh and vibrant flavor, while the garlic adds depth and richness. Plus, the chicken breasts stay moist and tender during the cooking process, thanks to the filling.
In conclusion, French-inspired recipes featuring herbs are a great way to add flavor and health benefits to your meals. From herb-crusted salmon to mushroom and herb quiche, these recipes showcase the versatility and complexity of herbs in French cuisine. Whether you're looking for a healthy and flavorful meal or an elegant and impressive dish, these recipes are sure to please. So, go ahead and experiment with different herbs and flavors to create your own French-inspired masterpieces in the kitchen!

18. Herb-infused Spanish and Mediterranean Dishes

Spanish and Mediterranean cuisine is known for its bold flavors and use of fresh herbs. Herbs play a crucial role in these cuisines, adding depth, flavor, and health benefits to dishes. In this chapter, we'll explore some herb-infused Spanish and Mediterranean dishes that are easy to prepare and bursting with flavor.

Herb-Infused Spanish and Mediterranean Dishes

Gazpacho

Gazpacho is a cold soup that originated in Andalusia, Spain. This refreshing soup is made with tomatoes, cucumber, bell pepper, garlic, and bread crumbs, and is typically served with a drizzle of olive oil and a sprinkle of fresh herbs.

Ingredients:

- 4 large ripe tomatoes
- 1 cucumber
- 1 red bell pepper
- 1/2 red onion
- 2 garlic cloves
- 2 tablespoons sherry vinegar
- 1/4 cup extra-virgin olive oil
- 2 cups stale bread, torn into small pieces
- 1/2 teaspoon salt
- Freshly ground black pepper
- 1/4 cup chopped fresh herbs (parsley, cilantro, or basil)

Instructions:

Roughly chop the tomatoes, cucumber, bell pepper, and red onion and place them in a blender.

Add the garlic, sherry vinegar, olive oil, and bread crumbs to the blender.

Blend the ingredients until smooth.

Season the gazpacho with salt and pepper.

Chill the gazpacho in the refrigerator for at least 2 hours.

To serve, drizzle the gazpacho with olive oil and sprinkle with fresh herbs.

Grilled Herb-Crusted Salmon

This grilled herb-crusted salmon is a healthy and flavorful way to incorporate herbs into your diet. The combination of fresh herbs and lemon juice gives the salmon a bright and tangy flavor that complements the richness of the fish.

Ingredients:

- 4 salmon fillets (6 ounces each)
- 1/4 cup chopped fresh herbs (parsley, thyme, and rosemary)
- 2 cloves garlic, minced
- 1/4 cup extra-virgin olive oil
- Juice of 1 lemon
- Salt and freshly ground black pepper

Instructions:

Preheat the grill to medium-high heat.

In a small bowl, mix together the herbs, garlic, olive oil, and lemon juice.

Season the salmon fillets with salt and pepper.

Brush the herb mixture over the salmon fillets.

Place the salmon fillets on the grill and cook for 5-6 minutes on each side, or until cooked through.

Herb-Marinated Chicken Skewers

These herb-marinated chicken skewers are a great addition to any summer barbecue or weeknight meal. The marinade is made with fresh herbs, lemon juice, and olive oil, which infuses the chicken with a bold and bright flavor.

Ingredients:

- 1 1/2 pounds boneless, skinless chicken breasts
- 1/4 cup chopped fresh herbs (rosemary, thyme, and oregano)
- 2 cloves garlic, minced
- Juice of 1 lemon
- 1/4 cup extra-virgin olive oil
- Salt and freshly ground black pepper
- Wooden skewers

Instructions:

Cut the chicken breasts into bite-sized pieces and place them in a large bowl.

In a small bowl, mix together the herbs, garlic, lemon juice, and olive oil.

Pour the herb mixture over the chicken and toss to coat.

Cover the bowl with plastic wrap and refrigerate for at least 30 minutes, or up to 2 hours.

Soak the wooden skewers in water for at least 30 minutes to prevent them from burning on the grill.
Thread the chicken onto the skewers.
Preheat the grill to medium-high heat.
Season the chicken skewers with salt and pepper.
Grill the chicken skewers for 8-10 minutes, turning occasionally, or until cooked through.

Herb and Lemon Roasted Potatoes

These herb and lemon roasted potatoes are a simple yet flavorful side dish that pairs well with a variety of main courses. The combination of fresh herbs and lemon juice gives the potatoes a bright and tangy flavor.

Ingredients:

- 2 pounds small potatoes (such as baby Yukon gold or fingerling)
- 1/4 cup chopped fresh herbs (rosemary, thyme, and oregano)
- 2 cloves garlic, minced
- 1/4 cup extra-virgin olive oil
- Juice and zest of 1 lemon
- Salt and freshly ground black pepper

Instructions:

Preheat the oven to 400°F.
Cut the potatoes in half lengthwise and place them in a large bowl.
In a small bowl, mix together the herbs, garlic, olive oil, lemon juice, and lemon zest.
Pour the herb mixture over the potatoes and toss to coat.
Season the potatoes with salt and pepper.
Transfer the potatoes to a large baking sheet.
Roast the potatoes in the oven for 25-30 minutes, or until golden brown and tender.

Herb and Feta Stuffed Chicken Breast

This herb and feta stuffed chicken breast is an impressive and flavorful main course that's perfect for entertaining. The combination of fresh herbs and tangy feta cheese elevates the chicken to a whole new level.

Ingredients:

- 4 boneless, skinless chicken breasts
- 1/2 cup crumbled feta cheese

- 1/4 cup chopped fresh herbs (parsley, thyme, and rosemary)
- 2 cloves garlic, minced
- 2 tablespoons extra-virgin olive oil
- Salt and freshly ground black pepper

Instructions:

Preheat the oven to 375°F.

In a small bowl, mix together the feta cheese, herbs, garlic, and olive oil.

Season the chicken breasts with salt and pepper.

Cut a slit lengthwise into the thickest part of each chicken breast, creating a pocket for the stuffing.

Stuff each chicken breast with the herb and feta mixture, using toothpicks to secure the opening.

Heat a large oven-safe skillet over medium-high heat.

Add the chicken breasts to the skillet and cook for 2-3 minutes on each side, or until golden brown.

Transfer the skillet to the oven and bake for 20-25 minutes, or until the chicken is cooked through.

In conclusion, spanish and Mediterranean cuisine is known for its bold and flavorful dishes that feature a variety of fresh herbs. These herb-infused recipes are not only delicious but also offer numerous health benefits. Incorporating fresh herbs into your cooking is an easy way to add flavor and nutrition to your meals. We hope you enjoy these herb-infused Spanish and Mediterranean dishes and experiment with other herb combinations in your own cooking.

19. Herb-infused Asian-inspired Dishes

Asian cuisine is known for its unique flavors and aroma, which are derived from the use of a variety of herbs and spices. From fragrant lemongrass to pungent ginger, herbs play a crucial role in many Asian-inspired dishes. In this chapter, we'll explore some of the most popular herb-infused Asian-inspired dishes that are easy to make and packed with flavor.

Thai Basil Chicken

Thai basil chicken is a classic dish that's popular in Thai cuisine. The dish is made with chicken, Thai basil, and a variety of other herbs and spices, making it a flavorful and aromatic dish.

Ingredients:

- 1 pound boneless, skinless chicken breast or thigh, cut into bite-sized pieces
- 1 tablespoon vegetable oil
- 3 cloves garlic, minced
- 2 Thai chilies, chopped (optional)
- 1/2 cup Thai basil leaves
- 1/4 cup chopped scallions
- 2 tablespoons fish sauce
- 1 tablespoon soy sauce
- 1 tablespoon oyster sauce
- 1 teaspoon sugar

Instructions:

Heat the oil in a wok or large skillet over high heat.

Add the garlic and chilies (if using) and stir-fry for 10 seconds.

Add the chicken and stir-fry until browned, about 2-3 minutes.

Add the fish sauce, soy sauce, oyster sauce, and sugar to the wok and stir-fry for another minute.

Add the Thai basil leaves and scallions and stir-fry for another 30 seconds.

Serve over rice or noodles.

Lemongrass and Ginger Broth

Lemongrass and ginger broth is a light and refreshing soup that's perfect for a starter or a light lunch. The broth is infused with lemongrass, ginger, and other herbs and spices, giving it a zesty and aromatic flavor.

Ingredients:

- 4 cups chicken or vegetable broth
- 2 stalks lemongrass, bruised and chopped
- 2-inch piece of fresh ginger, sliced
- 4 cloves garlic, smashed
- 2 kaffir lime leaves
- 1/4 cup chopped cilantro
- 1 tablespoon fish sauce
- 1 tablespoon soy sauce
- Salt and freshly ground black pepper

Instructions:

In a large pot, bring the broth to a boil.
Add the lemongrass, ginger, garlic, and kaffir lime leaves to the pot.
Reduce the heat to medium-low and let the broth simmer for 15-20 minutes.
Strain the broth to remove the solids.
Add the cilantro, fish sauce, soy sauce, salt, and pepper to the broth and stir to combine.
Serve hot.

Green Curry Shrimp

Green curry shrimp is a spicy and flavorful dish that's popular in Thai cuisine. The dish is made with green curry paste, coconut milk, and a variety of herbs and spices, giving it a complex and aromatic flavor.

Ingredients:

- 1 pound large shrimp, peeled and deveined
- 2 tablespoons vegetable oil
- 2 tablespoons green curry paste
- 1 can (13.5 oz) coconut milk
- 1/2 cup chopped basil leaves
- 1/4 cup chopped cilantro leaves
- 1/4 cup chopped scallions
- 2 tablespoons fish sauce
- 1 tablespoon sugar

Instructions:

Heat the oil in a wok or large skillet over medium-high heat.
Add the green curry paste to the wok and stir-fry for 1 minute.

Add the shrimp to the wok and stir-fry until pink, about 3-4 minutes.
Add the coconut milk, basil, cilantro, scallions, fish sauce, and sugar to the wok and bring to a simmer.
Let the curry simmer for 5-7 minutes, or until the shrimp is fully cooked and the sauce has thickened slightly.
Serve over rice or noodles.

Ginger Garlic Bok Choy

Ginger garlic bok choy is a simple and healthy side dish that's perfect for any Asian-inspired meal. The dish is made with bok choy, garlic, ginger, and a few other seasonings, giving it a flavorful and aromatic taste.

Ingredients:

- 1 pound bok choy, washed and trimmed
- 2 tablespoons vegetable oil
- 2 cloves garlic, minced
- 1-inch piece of fresh ginger, grated
- 2 tablespoons soy sauce
- 1 tablespoon sesame oil
- 1/4 teaspoon red pepper flakes (optional)
- Salt and freshly ground black pepper

Instructions:

Cut the bok choy in half lengthwise.
In a large skillet, heat the vegetable oil over medium-high heat.
Add the garlic and ginger to the skillet and stir-fry for 30 seconds.
Add the bok choy to the skillet and stir-fry for 2-3 minutes.
Add the soy sauce, sesame oil, red pepper flakes (if using), salt, and pepper to the skillet and stir-fry for another minute.
Serve hot.

Vietnamese Pho

Vietnamese pho is a popular noodle soup that's packed with flavor and aromatic herbs. The dish is made with rice noodles, beef or chicken, and a variety of herbs and spices, giving it a complex and flavorful taste.

Ingredients:

- 8 cups beef or chicken broth
- 1 pound beef or chicken, thinly sliced
- 1 onion, sliced

- 2-inch piece of fresh ginger, sliced
- 2 cinnamon sticks
- 4 star anise
- 4 cloves
- 1 tablespoon fish sauce
- 1 tablespoon soy sauce
- 1 tablespoon sugar
- 1 package (14 oz) rice noodles
- 1/4 cup chopped cilantro
- 1/4 cup chopped basil leaves
- 1/4 cup chopped mint leaves
- 1/4 cup chopped scallions
- 1 lime, cut into wedges

Instructions:

In a large pot, bring the broth to a boil.
Add the onion, ginger, cinnamon sticks, star anise, and cloves to the pot.
Reduce the heat to low and let the broth simmer for 1 hour.
Strain the broth to remove the solids.
Add the fish sauce, soy sauce, and sugar to the broth and stir to combine.
Cook the rice noodles according to the package instructions.
Divide the noodles among 4-6 bowls.
Top the noodles with the sliced beef or chicken.
Pour the hot broth over the noodles and beef or chicken.
Garnish the soup with cilantro, basil, mint, scallions, and lime wedges.
Serve hot.

In conclusion, herbs play a crucial role in Asian-inspired cuisine, adding flavor and aroma to a variety of dishes. From lemongrass and ginger to Thai basil and cilantro, these herbs are used in a variety of ways to create complex and delicious flavors. The recipes in this chapter are just a few examples of how you can use herbs in your Asian-inspired cooking. Feel free to experiment with different herbs and ingredients to create your own unique dishes.

One of the best things about cooking with herbs is the health benefits they provide. Many of the herbs used in Asian cuisine have medicinal properties, such as anti-inflammatory and anti-bacterial effects. By incorporating herbs into your meals, you can not only add flavor but also promote overall health and well-being.

20. Bold and Flavorful Indian Recipes with Herbs

Indian cuisine is famous for its bold and flavorful dishes, and herbs play a vital role in creating these delicious recipes. Whether it's the fragrant curry leaves in a South Indian dish or the aromatic coriander in a North Indian dish, herbs are a crucial component in Indian cooking. In this chapter, we will explore the different herbs used in Indian cuisine and how they enhance the flavors of the dishes. We will also provide some delicious recipes that showcase the use of herbs in Indian cooking.

Herbs Used in Indian Cuisine

Coriander (Dhania): Coriander is one of the most commonly used herbs in Indian cuisine. It has a fresh, citrusy flavor that pairs well with spicy and savory dishes. Coriander is used both fresh and dried in Indian cooking, and it's often added to chutneys, curries, and marinades.

Cumin (Jeera): Cumin is another essential herb in Indian cuisine. It has a warm, earthy flavor and is often used in spice blends, such as garam masala and curry powder. Cumin is also added to soups, stews, and sautéed vegetables.

Turmeric (Haldi): Turmeric is a bright yellow herb that has a warm, slightly bitter flavor. It's used extensively in Indian cooking and is a key ingredient in curry powder. Turmeric is known for its anti-inflammatory properties and is often used in Ayurvedic medicine.

Curry Leaves: Curry leaves are a staple in South Indian cooking. They have a pungent, slightly bitter flavor and are added to curries, soups, and stews. Curry leaves are often sautéed with mustard seeds and other spices to create a flavorful seasoning.

Mint (Pudina): Mint is used in both sweet and savory dishes in Indian cuisine. It has a cool, refreshing flavor and is often added to chutneys, raitas, and biryanis. Mint leaves can also be steeped in hot water to make a refreshing tea.

Fenugreek (Methi): Fenugreek has a slightly bitter, nutty flavor and is often used in spice blends, such as garam masala. Fenugreek leaves are also used in curries and stews, and the seeds are often toasted and ground to add flavor to dishes.

Coriander Chicken Curry

This spicy chicken curry is made with a fragrant coriander paste and a blend of spices. It's perfect for a cozy dinner at home or for entertaining guests.

Ingredients:

- 4 boneless, skinless chicken breasts, cut into bite-sized pieces
- 1 large onion, chopped
- 2 cloves garlic, minced
- 1 tbsp ginger paste
- 1 tbsp coriander powder
- 1 tsp cumin powder
- 1 tsp turmeric powder
- 1 tsp chili powder
- Salt to taste
- 1 cup fresh coriander leaves, chopped
- 2 tbsp oil
- 1 cup water

Instructions:

In a large pot, heat the oil over medium-high heat. Add the onions, garlic, and ginger paste and sauté until the onions are translucent.

Add the chicken pieces and cook until browned on all sides.

Add the coriander powder, cumin powder, turmeric powder, chili powder, and salt. Stir well and cook for 1-2 minutes.

Add the chopped coriander leaves and water. Cover and simmer for 20-25 minutes or until the chicken is cooked through.

Serve hot with rice or naan bread.

Mint Chutney

This tangy and refreshing chutney is a classic condiment in Indian cuisine. It's easy to make and pairs well with grilled meats, sandwiches, and samosas.

Ingredients:

- 2 cups fresh mint leaves
- 1 cup fresh coriander leaves
- 1 small onion, chopped
- 1-2 green chilies, chopped
- 1 inch piece of ginger, peeled and chopped
- 1-2 garlic cloves, chopped
- 1 tsp cumin powder

- Salt to taste
- 1-2 tbsp lemon juice

Water as needed

Instructions:

In a food processor or blender, combine the mint leaves, coriander leaves, onion, green chilies, ginger, garlic, cumin powder, and salt. Pulse until everything is well blended.

Gradually add water, 1 tablespoon at a time, until the mixture becomes smooth and has a chutney-like consistency.

Transfer the chutney to a serving bowl and stir in the lemon juice.

Serve with your favorite dish.

Fenugreek and Potato Curry

This hearty curry is made with potatoes and fenugreek leaves. It's a comforting dish that's perfect for a chilly evening.

Ingredients:

- 3-4 medium-sized potatoes, peeled and cubed
- 2 cups fresh fenugreek leaves, chopped
- 1 large onion, chopped
- 2-3 garlic cloves, minced
- 1 inch piece of ginger, peeled and minced
- 1 tsp cumin seeds
- 1 tsp coriander powder
- 1 tsp turmeric powder
- 1 tsp chili powder
- Salt to taste
- 2 tbsp oil
- 1 cup water

Instructions:

In a large pot, heat the oil over medium-high heat. Add the cumin seeds and sauté until they start to splutter.

Add the onions, garlic, and ginger and sauté until the onions are translucent.

Add the potatoes and sauté for 5-7 minutes or until they are lightly browned.

Add the coriander powder, turmeric powder, chili powder, and salt. Stir well and cook for 1-2 minutes.

Add the fenugreek leaves and water. Cover and simmer for 20-25 minutes or until the potatoes are cooked through.
Serve hot with rice or naan bread.
In conclusion, Indian cuisine is known for its bold and flavorful dishes, and herbs play a crucial role in creating these delicious recipes. From the fresh citrusy flavor of coriander to the warm earthy taste of cumin, each herb adds a unique flavor profile to the dish. By incorporating herbs into your cooking, you can elevate the flavors of your dishes and create a culinary experience that's both delicious and healthy. So go ahead and experiment with different herbs in your Indian dishes, and let your taste buds take a journey to the vibrant flavors of India.

21. Making the Perfect Herb-infused Sauce

Sauces are an essential part of many cuisines around the world, and adding herbs to your sauce can take your dish to the next level. Herb-infused sauces are a fantastic way to add flavor, aroma, and health benefits to your dishes. In this chapter, we'll discuss how to make the perfect herb-infused sauce and provide some examples of sauces that can be enhanced with herbs.

Choosing Your Herbs

The first step to making a great herb-infused sauce is choosing the right herbs. When selecting herbs, consider the flavor profile of the dish you're making. For example, if you're making an Italian dish, you may want to use basil, oregano, or rosemary. For a Mexican dish, cilantro, cumin, or chili peppers may be a better fit.

Fresh herbs are ideal for sauces because they have a vibrant flavor and aroma. However, if fresh herbs are not available, you can use dried herbs. Dried herbs are more potent than fresh herbs, so use them sparingly.

Preparing Your Herbs

Once you've chosen your herbs, it's time to prepare them. Rinse the herbs thoroughly and pat them dry with a paper towel. Remove any stems or woody parts, and finely chop the leaves.

If you're using dried herbs, you don't need to chop them, but you can rub them between your fingers to release their flavor.

Infusing Your Sauce with Herbs

There are several ways to infuse your sauce with herbs. The most common methods are steeping, simmering, or blending.

Steeping: This method involves adding the herbs to a hot liquid and letting them steep for several minutes. Steeping is best for delicate herbs like mint, basil, and cilantro.

Simmering: Simmering involves adding the herbs to a sauce and letting them simmer for an extended period. Simmering is ideal for heartier herbs like thyme, rosemary, and oregano.

Blending: This method involves blending the herbs with the sauce to create a smooth, flavorful sauce. Blending is ideal for sauces that require a smooth texture, like pesto.

Examples of Herb-Infused Sauces

Tomato Sauce with Basil

Tomato sauce is a classic Italian sauce that's delicious on pasta, pizza, or as a dipping sauce. Adding fresh basil to tomato sauce creates a refreshing and aromatic sauce that's perfect for summer.

Ingredients:

- 1 can of crushed tomatoes
- 2 cloves of garlic, minced
- 1 small onion, chopped
- 1/4 cup of fresh basil leaves, chopped
- 2 tablespoons of olive oil
- Salt and pepper to taste

Instructions:

In a medium saucepan, heat the olive oil over medium heat. Add the garlic and onion and sauté until they are translucent.

Add the crushed tomatoes and bring the sauce to a simmer.

Add the chopped basil leaves and simmer the sauce for 10-15 minutes.

Season the sauce with salt and pepper to taste.

Serve the sauce over pasta or as a dipping sauce.

Chimichurri Sauce

Chimichurri is a tangy and garlicky sauce from Argentina that's traditionally served with grilled meats. Adding fresh parsley and oregano to the sauce creates a bold and flavorful sauce that's perfect for grilled steaks or chicken.

Ingredients:

- 1 cup of fresh parsley, chopped
- 1/4 cup of fresh oregano, chopped
- 1/4 cup of red wine vinegar
- 3 garlic cloves, minced
- 1/2 teaspoon of red pepper flakes
- 1/2 cup of olive oil
- Salt and pepper to taste

Instructions:

In a medium bowl, combine the chopped parsley and oregano.

Add the minced garlic, red pepper flakes, and red wine vinegar to the bowl and stir to combine.

Slowly drizzle in the olive oil while whisking the sauce until it emulsifies.
Season the sauce with salt and pepper to taste.
Serve the chimichurri sauce with grilled meats.

Peanut Sauce

Peanut sauce is a popular sauce in Southeast Asian cuisine that's often served with noodles, chicken, or vegetables. Adding fresh ginger and cilantro to the sauce creates a flavorful and aromatic sauce that's perfect for stir-fry dishes.

Ingredients:

- 1/2 cup of creamy peanut butter
- 1/4 cup of soy sauce
- 2 tablespoons of honey
- 2 tablespoons of rice vinegar
- 1 tablespoon of grated fresh ginger
- 1/4 cup of fresh cilantro, chopped
- 1 clove of garlic, minced
- 1/4 teaspoon of red pepper flakes (optional)
- 1/4 cup of water

Instructions:

In a medium bowl, whisk together the peanut butter, soy sauce, honey, and rice vinegar.
Add the grated ginger, chopped cilantro, minced garlic, and red pepper flakes (if using) to the bowl and stir to combine.
Slowly whisk in the water to thin the sauce to your desired consistency.
Season the sauce with salt and pepper to taste.
Serve the peanut sauce with noodles, chicken, or vegetables.
Tips for Making the Perfect Herb-Infused Sauce
Start with fresh herbs for the best flavor and aroma.
Use a gentle heat to infuse the herbs into the sauce to prevent burning or bitterness.
Taste the sauce as you go and adjust the seasoning as needed.
Store leftover herb-infused sauce in an airtight container in the refrigerator for up to a week.
Experiment with different herbs and sauces to create your own unique flavor combinations.

In conclusion, herb-infused sauces are an excellent way to add flavor, aroma, and health benefits to your dishes. By choosing the right herbs, preparing them properly, and infusing them into your sauce, you can create a bold and flavorful sauce that will elevate any dish. Whether you're making a classic tomato sauce or a tangy peanut sauce, herbs are a versatile and essential ingredient that can take your sauce to the next level.

22. Desserts with a Hint of Herb Flavor

Herbs are typically used in savory dishes to enhance their flavor, but did you know that they can also be used in desserts? Adding a hint of herb flavor to your sweet treats can take them to the next level and add a unique and unexpected twist. In this chapter, we'll explore the world of desserts with a hint of herb flavor.

Before we dive into specific dessert recipes, it's important to note that not all herbs are created equal when it comes to pairing them with sweets. Some herbs, like rosemary and thyme, have a strong, savory flavor that may not work well in desserts. Other herbs, like lavender and mint, have a more delicate and floral flavor that can complement the sweetness of desserts.

When using herbs in desserts, it's best to start with small amounts and adjust as needed. A little goes a long way, and you don't want to overpower the other flavors in your dessert. It's also important to use fresh herbs whenever possible, as dried herbs can be too strong and overpowering.

Now, let's get into some delicious dessert recipes with a hint of herb flavor!

Lavender Honey Panna Cotta

Panna cotta is a classic Italian dessert that is creamy and silky in texture. Adding lavender and honey gives it a unique and delicate flavor that pairs perfectly with the richness of the cream.

Ingredients:

- 2 cups heavy cream
- 1/4 cup honey
- 1 tbsp dried lavender
- 1 tsp vanilla extract
- 2 tsp gelatin powder
- 2 tbsp cold water

Instructions:

In a saucepan, heat the heavy cream, honey, and dried lavender over medium heat until it just begins to simmer.

Remove the saucepan from heat and stir in the vanilla extract.

In a separate bowl, sprinkle the gelatin powder over the cold water and let it sit for 5 minutes until it becomes soft.

Whisk the gelatin mixture into the cream mixture until fully incorporated.
Strain the mixture through a fine-mesh sieve to remove the lavender buds.
Pour the mixture into ramekins or small cups and refrigerate for at least 2 hours or until set.
Serve chilled with fresh berries or whipped cream.

Mint Chocolate Chip Ice Cream

Mint and chocolate are a classic flavor combination, but adding fresh mint to your homemade ice cream takes it to the next level. This recipe uses fresh mint leaves to infuse the cream with flavor, creating a refreshing and delicious treat.

Ingredients:

- 2 cups heavy cream
- 1 cup whole milk
- 3/4 cup granulated sugar
- 1/4 cup fresh mint leaves, chopped
- 4 egg yolks
- 1 tsp vanilla extract
- 1/2 cup chocolate chips

Instructions:

In a saucepan, heat the heavy cream, whole milk, granulated sugar, and chopped mint leaves over medium heat until it just begins to simmer.
Remove the saucepan from heat and let the mixture steep for 20-30 minutes.
In a separate bowl, whisk together the egg yolks and vanilla extract.
Slowly pour the cream mixture into the egg yolk mixture, whisking constantly, until fully incorporated.
Pour the mixture back into the saucepan and heat over medium heat, stirring constantly, until it thickens and coats the back of a spoon.
Remove the saucepan from heat and let it cool to room temperature.
Pour the mixture into an ice cream maker and churn according to the manufacturer's instructions.
Stir in the chocolate chips and transfer the ice cream to a freezer-safe container.
Freeze the ice cream for at least 4 hours or until firm.
Serve with additional fresh mint leaves and chocolate shavings, if desired.

Lemon Thyme Shortbread Cookies

Shortbread cookies are a classic dessert that are buttery and crumbly in texture. Adding lemon and thyme gives them a fresh and herbaceous flavor that is perfect for spring and summer.

Ingredients:

- 1 cup unsalted butter, at room temperature
- 1/2 cup powdered sugar
- 2 cups all-purpose flour
- 1/4 tsp salt
- 1 tbsp fresh thyme leaves, chopped
- Zest of 1 lemon

Instructions:

Preheat the oven to 350°F (175°C) and line a baking sheet with parchment paper.

In a large bowl, cream together the butter and powdered sugar until light and fluffy.

In a separate bowl, whisk together the flour and salt.

Gradually add the flour mixture to the butter mixture, mixing until fully incorporated.

Stir in the chopped thyme leaves and lemon zest.

Roll the dough into a log shape and wrap in plastic wrap.

Chill the dough in the refrigerator for at least 30 minutes or until firm.

Slice the dough into 1/4-inch-thick rounds and place them on the prepared baking sheet.

Bake for 12-15 minutes or until the edges are lightly golden.

Let the cookies cool on the baking sheet for 5 minutes before transferring them to a wire rack to cool completely.

Basil Strawberry Shortcake

Shortcake is a classic dessert that typically features sweet, juicy strawberries and whipped cream. Adding fresh basil to the shortcake biscuits gives them a unique and herbaceous flavor that complements the sweetness of the strawberries.

Ingredients:

For the shortcake biscuits:

- 2 cups all-purpose flour
- 2 tbsp granulated sugar

- 1 tbsp baking powder
- 1/2 tsp salt
- 1/2 cup unsalted butter, cold and cubed
- 1/4 cup fresh basil leaves, chopped
- 3/4 cup whole milk
- 1 egg, beaten

For the strawberries:

- 2 cups fresh strawberries, hulled and sliced
- 2 tbsp granulated sugar
- 1 tbsp fresh basil leaves, chopped
- For the whipped cream:
- 1 cup heavy cream
- 2 tbsp powdered sugar
- 1 tsp vanilla extract

Instructions:

Preheat the oven to 425°F (220°C) and line a baking sheet with parchment paper.

In a large bowl, whisk together the flour, granulated sugar, baking powder, and salt.

Add the cold, cubed butter to the flour mixture and use a pastry cutter or your hands to cut it into the flour until it resembles coarse crumbs.

Stir in the chopped basil leaves.

In a separate bowl, whisk together the whole milk and beaten egg.

Gradually add the milk mixture to the flour mixture, stirring until just combined.

Turn the dough out onto a lightly floured surface and knead it gently until it comes together.

Roll the dough out to 1/2-inch thickness and use a biscuit cutter or round cookie cutter to cut out 6 biscuits.

Place the biscuits on the prepared baking sheet and bake for 15-18 minutes or until golden brown.

While the biscuits are baking, prepare the strawberries. In a bowl, toss the sliced strawberries with the granulated sugar and chopped basil leaves.

In a separate bowl, whip the heavy cream, powdered sugar, and vanilla extract together until stiff peaks form.

To assemble the shortcakes, slice each biscuit in half horizontally.
Place a spoonful of the strawberry mixture on the bottom half of each biscuit.
Top the strawberries with a dollop of whipped cream.
Place the top half of the biscuit on top of the whipped cream.
Serve immediately and enjoy!
In conclusion, herbs can be a wonderful addition to desserts, adding a unique and fresh flavor that can take your baking to the next level. Whether you're making an herbed fruit salad, a mint chocolate chip ice cream, or a basil strawberry shortcake, there are plenty of ways to incorporate herbs into your desserts.
Not only do herbs add flavor, but many of them also have health benefits as well. For example, mint can aid digestion, lavender can help reduce stress and anxiety, and thyme has antibacterial properties. So, not only will your desserts taste great, but they may also offer some health benefits as well.
So why not experiment with herbs in your next dessert recipe? Whether you're using fresh herbs from your garden or dried herbs from your pantry, the possibilities are endless. Get creative and see what delicious combinations you can come up with!

23. Herb-infused Cocktails and Beverages

Herbs are not just for cooking. They can add flavor, aroma, and health benefits to cocktails and other beverages. Whether you are hosting a party or enjoying a drink at home, herb-infused cocktails and beverages are a great way to impress your guests and enjoy the health benefits of herbs.

In this chapter, we will explore some of the most popular herbs used in cocktails and beverages and share some easy-to-follow recipes that you can try at home.

Mint

Mint is one of the most popular herbs used in cocktails and beverages. It has a refreshing taste and aroma that complements many drinks. Mint also has several health benefits, including improving digestion and reducing inflammation.

Mint Mojito

The Mint Mojito is a classic cocktail that is perfect for hot summer days. Here's how to make it:

Ingredients:

- 2 oz white rum
- 1 oz lime juice
- 1 oz simple syrup
- 8-10 fresh mint leaves
- Club soda
- Ice

Instructions:

Muddle the mint leaves in a cocktail shaker.

Add the white rum, lime juice, and simple syrup to the shaker.

Add ice to the shaker and shake well.

Strain the mixture into a glass filled with ice.

Top off the glass with club soda.

Garnish with a sprig of fresh mint and a lime wedge.

Lemon Balm

Lemon balm has a bright lemon flavor that is perfect for adding a citrusy twist to cocktails and other beverages. It is also known for its calming and soothing properties, making it a great choice for a relaxing drink.

Lemon Balm Martini

The Lemon Balm Martini is a refreshing cocktail that is perfect for any occasion. Here's how to make it:

Ingredients:

- 2 oz vodka
- 1 oz lemon juice
- 1 oz simple syrup
- 4-5 fresh lemon balm leaves
- Ice

Instructions:

Muddle the lemon balm leaves in a cocktail shaker.
Add the vodka, lemon juice, and simple syrup to the shaker.
Add ice to the shaker and shake well.
Strain the mixture into a chilled martini glass.
Garnish with a lemon twist and a sprig of fresh lemon balm.

Lavender

Lavender has a distinct floral flavor and aroma that is perfect for adding a unique twist to cocktails and other beverages. It is also known for its calming properties, making it a great choice for a relaxing drink.

Lavender Lemonade

Lavender Lemonade is a refreshing and relaxing drink that is perfect for hot summer days. Here's how to make it:

Ingredients:

- 1 cup freshly squeezed lemon juice
- 1 cup lavender simple syrup*
- 4 cups water
- Ice
- Fresh lavender sprigs, for garnish

Instructions:

In a large pitcher, combine the lemon juice, lavender simple syrup, and water.
Stir well to combine.
Add ice to the pitcher.
Pour the Lavender Lemonade into glasses and garnish with fresh lavender sprigs.

Lavender Simple Syrup: In a medium saucepan, combine 1 cup water, 1 cup sugar, and 1/4 cup dried culinary lavender. Bring to a boil over medium-high heat, stirring until the sugar dissolves. Reduce the heat to low and simmer for 5-10 minutes, until the lavender flavor has infused into the syrup. Remove from heat and let cool. Strain out the lavender and store the syrup in an airtight container in the refrigerator.

Rosemary has a strong, woody flavor that pairs well with savory and sweet drinks. It is also known for its antioxidant and anti-inflammatory properties.

Rosemary Gin Fizz

The Rosemary Gin Fizz is a refreshing and herbaceous cocktail that is perfect for any occasion. Here's how to make it:

Ingredients:

- 2 oz gin
- 1 oz lemon juice
- 1 oz rosemary simple syrup*
- Club soda
- Rosemary sprig, for garnish
- Ice

Instructions:

In a cocktail shaker, combine the gin, lemon juice, and rosemary simple syrup.
Add ice to the shaker and shake well.
Strain the mixture into a glass filled with ice.
Top off the glass with club soda.
Garnish with a sprig of fresh rosemary.

Rosemary Simple Syrup: In a medium saucepan, combine 1 cup water, 1 cup sugar, and 2-3 sprigs of fresh rosemary. Bring to a boil over medium-high heat, stirring until the sugar dissolves. Reduce the heat to low and simmer for 5-10 minutes, until the rosemary flavor has infused into the syrup. Remove from heat and let cool. Strain out the rosemary and store the syrup in an airtight container in the refrigerator.

Thyme

Thyme has a slightly minty and lemony flavor that pairs well with many cocktails and beverages. It is also known for its antiseptic and antifungal properties.

Thyme Lemonade

Thyme Lemonade is a refreshing and flavorful drink that is perfect for hot summer days. Here's how to make it:

Ingredients:

- 1 cup freshly squeezed lemon juice
- 1 cup thyme simple syrup*
- 4 cups water
- Ice
- Fresh thyme sprigs, for garnish

Instructions:

In a large pitcher, combine the lemon juice, thyme simple syrup, and water.
Stir well to combine.
Add ice to the pitcher.
Pour the Thyme Lemonade into glasses and garnish with fresh thyme sprigs.
Thyme Simple Syrup: In a medium saucepan, combine 1 cup water, 1 cup sugar, and 2-3 sprigs of fresh thyme. Bring to a boil over medium-high heat, stirring until the sugar dissolves. Reduce the heat to low and simmer for 5-10 minutes, until the thyme flavor has infused into the syrup. Remove from heat and let cool. Strain out the thyme and store the syrup in an airtight container in the refrigerator.

In conclusion, herb-infused cocktails and beverages are a great way to add flavor, aroma, and health benefits to your drinks. From the classic Mint Mojito to the herbaceous Rosemary Gin Fizz, there are endless possibilities when it comes to using herbs in your drinks. Experiment with different herbs and flavors to create your own unique and delicious cocktails and beverages.

24. Herb-Infused Infused Oils and Vinegars

Herb-Infused Oils and Vinegars have been used for centuries to add flavor and depth to dishes. They are simple to make, and the possibilities are endless. In this chapter, we will explore the different herbs and techniques to make herb-infused oils and vinegars to elevate your cooking game.

Choosing the Right Herbs

When making herb-infused oils and vinegars, it is important to choose the right herbs. Not all herbs are created equal, and some work better with oils and others with vinegars. Here are some herbs to consider:

Herbs for Infused Oils:

- Rosemary
- Thyme
- Basil
- Oregano
- Sage
- Garlic

Herbs for Infused Vinegars:

- Tarragon
- Dill
- Basil
- Mint
- Rosemary
- Thyme

Techniques for Making Herb-Infused Oils and Vinegars

There are two methods for making herb-infused oils and vinegars: cold infusion and hot infusion.

Cold Infusion

Cold infusion is a simple method of infusing herbs into oil or vinegar. This method takes longer but results in a more subtle flavor. Here's how to make a cold-infused herb oil or vinegar:

Ingredients:

- 1 cup oil or vinegar
- 1/2 cup fresh herbs

Instructions:

Wash and dry the herbs thoroughly.

In a glass jar, combine the herbs and oil or vinegar.

Seal the jar and let it sit in a cool, dark place for 1-2 weeks.

After 1-2 weeks, strain out the herbs and store the infused oil or vinegar in a clean glass jar.

Hot Infusion

Hot infusion is a quicker method for infusing herbs into oil or vinegar. This method results in a more intense flavor. Here's how to make a hot-infused herb oil or vinegar:

Ingredients:

- 1 cup oil or vinegar
- 1/2 cup fresh herbs

Instructions:

Wash and dry the herbs thoroughly.

In a saucepan, heat the oil or vinegar over low heat until warm.

Add the herbs to the warm oil or vinegar.

Let the mixture simmer over low heat for 10-15 minutes.

After 10-15 minutes, remove the saucepan from the heat and let it cool.

Strain out the herbs and store the infused oil or vinegar in a clean glass jar.

Tips for Making Herb-Infused Oils and Vinegars

Use high-quality oils and vinegars to ensure the best results.

Make sure to wash and dry the herbs thoroughly before using them.

Use fresh herbs for the best flavor.

Store the infused oils and vinegars in a cool, dark place to preserve their flavor.

Label the jars with the name of the herb and the date of infusion to keep track of their freshness.

Recipes for Herb-Infused Oils and Vinegars

Here are two recipes for herb-infused oils and vinegars to get you started:

Rosemary Infused Olive Oil

Rosemary Infused Olive Oil is a delicious and versatile oil that can be used for marinades, dressings, and dipping sauces.

Ingredients:

- 1 cup extra-virgin olive oil
- 1/2 cup fresh rosemary

Instructions:

Wash and dry the rosemary thoroughly.

In a glass jar, combine the rosemary and olive oil.

Seal the jar and let it sit in a cool, dark place for 1-2 weeks.

After 1-2 weeks, strain out the rosemary and store the infused olive oil in a clean glass jar.

Tarragon Infused White Wine Vinegar

Tarragon Infused White Wine Vinegar is a tangy and flavorful vinegar that can be used in salad dressings, marinades, and sauces.

Ingredients:

- 1 cup white wine vinegar
- 1/2 cup fresh tarragon

Instructions:

Wash and dry the tarragon thoroughly.

In a saucepan, heat the white wine vinegar over low heat until warm.

Add the tarragon to the warm vinegar.

Let the mixture simmer over low heat for 10-15 minutes.

After 10-15 minutes, remove the saucepan from the heat and let it cool.

Strain out the tarragon and store the infused white wine vinegar in a clean glass jar.

In conclusion, herb-infused oils and vinegars are easy to make and add a delicious and healthy flavor to dishes. Experiment with different herbs and techniques to find your favorite flavor combinations. Remember to use high-quality oils and vinegars, and label the jars with the name of the herb and the date of infusion to keep track of their freshness. With these tips and recipes, you'll be making herb-infused oils and vinegars like a pro in no time.

25. Quick and Easy Herb-infused Dressings

Herb-infused dressings are a quick and easy way to add flavor and nutrition to your salads and vegetables. They can be made with a variety of herbs, oils, and vinegars, and can be customized to your taste preferences. In this chapter, we will explore some quick and easy herb-infused dressing recipes that are perfect for any meal.

Choosing the Right Herbs

When making herb-infused dressings, it is important to choose the right herbs. Different herbs have different flavor profiles, and some work better with certain dressings than others. Here are some herbs to consider:

Basil: adds a sweet, slightly peppery flavor that works well with olive oil and balsamic vinegar.

Dill: adds a fresh, tangy flavor that works well with yogurt-based dressings.

Mint: adds a cool, refreshing flavor that works well with lemon-based dressings.

Cilantro: adds a fresh, zesty flavor that works well with lime-based dressings.

Rosemary: adds a woodsy, aromatic flavor that works well with honey-based dressings.

Quick and Easy Herb-Infused Dressing Recipes

Basil Vinaigrette

This classic dressing is perfect for any salad or vegetable. It's simple to make and can be stored in the fridge for up to a week.

Ingredients:

- 1/4 cup extra-virgin olive oil
- 2 tablespoons balsamic vinegar
- 1 garlic clove, minced
- 1 tablespoon honey
- 1/4 cup fresh basil, chopped

Salt and pepper to taste

Instructions:

In a small bowl, whisk together the olive oil, balsamic vinegar, garlic, and honey.

Add the chopped basil and stir to combine.

Season with salt and pepper to taste.

Dill Yogurt Dressing

This creamy dressing is perfect for adding a tangy flavor to your salads or veggies. It's made with Greek yogurt, which adds protein and probiotics to your meal.

Ingredients:

- 1/2 cup plain Greek yogurt
- 2 tablespoons fresh dill, chopped
- 1 tablespoon lemon juice
- 1 garlic clove, minced
- Salt and pepper to taste

Instructions:

In a small bowl, whisk together the Greek yogurt, dill, lemon juice, and garlic.
Season with salt and pepper to taste.

Mint-Lemon Dressing

This refreshing dressing is perfect for adding a cool flavor to your salads or veggies. It's made with fresh mint and lemon juice, which add a burst of flavor and nutrition to your meal.

Ingredients:

- 1/4 cup extra-virgin olive oil
- 2 tablespoons lemon juice
- 1 garlic clove, minced
- 1 tablespoon honey
- 1/4 cup fresh mint, chopped
- Salt and pepper to taste

Instructions:

In a small bowl, whisk together the olive oil, lemon juice, garlic, and honey.
Add the chopped mint and stir to combine.
Season with salt and pepper to taste.

Cilantro-Lime Dressing

This zesty dressing is perfect for adding a fresh flavor to your salads or veggies. It's made with fresh cilantro and lime juice, which add a burst of flavor and nutrition to your meal.

Ingredients:

- 1/4 cup extra-virgin olive oil
- 2 tablespoons lime juice
- 1 garlic clove, minced

- 1 tablespoon honey
- 1/4 cup fresh cilantro, chopped
- Salt and pepper to taste

Instructions:

In a small bowl, whisk together the olive oil, lime juice, garlic, and honey

Add the chopped cilantro and stir to combine.

Season with salt and pepper to taste.

Rosemary-Honey Dressing

This flavorful dressing is perfect for adding a sweet and aromatic flavor to your salads or veggies. It's made with fresh rosemary and honey, which add a unique and delicious flavor to your meal.

Ingredients:

- 1/4 cup extra-virgin olive oil
- 2 tablespoons apple cider vinegar
- 1 garlic clove, minced
- 1 tablespoon honey
- 1 tablespoon fresh rosemary, chopped
- Salt and pepper to taste

Instructions:

In a small bowl, whisk together the olive oil, apple cider vinegar, garlic, and honey.

Add the chopped rosemary and stir to combine.

Season with salt and pepper to taste.

Tips for Making Herb-Infused Dressings

Use fresh herbs: Fresh herbs have more flavor and nutrition than dried herbs, so it's always best to use fresh herbs when making herb-infused dressings.

Use high-quality oils and vinegars: High-quality oils and vinegars will have a better flavor and will be healthier for you. Look for extra-virgin olive oil and unfiltered apple cider vinegar.

Customize to your taste: Feel free to experiment with different herbs, oils, and vinegars to create your perfect dressing. You can also adjust the amount of each ingredient to your taste preferences.

Store in the fridge: Herb-infused dressings can be stored in the fridge for up to a week. Just make sure to store them in an airtight container and give them a good shake before using.

In conclusion, herb-infused dressings are a quick and easy way to add flavor and nutrition to your salads and veggies. With a few simple ingredients and some fresh herbs, you can create delicious and healthy dressings that will take your meal to the next level. Try out these recipes and tips, and see how easy it is to make your own herb-infused dressings.

26. Herb-infused Butters and Spreads

Herb-infused butters and spreads are a great way to add flavor and nutrition to your meals. They are easy to make and can be used in a variety of ways, from spreading on bread to topping off a steak or grilled veggies. In this chapter, we will explore different recipes and tips for making delicious herb-infused butters and spreads.

Garlic-Herb Butter

This classic butter is perfect for adding flavor to your steak or spreading on bread. It's made with fresh garlic and herbs, which add a delicious flavor and aroma to your dish.

Ingredients:

- 1 stick unsalted butter, room temperature
- 1 garlic clove, minced
- 1 tablespoon fresh parsley, chopped
- 1 tablespoon fresh chives, chopped
- Salt and pepper to taste

Instructions:

In a small bowl, combine the butter, garlic, parsley, and chives.

Mix well until all ingredients are fully incorporated.

Season with salt and pepper to taste.

Transfer the butter to a piece of parchment paper and shape into a log.

Wrap the parchment paper around the butter and twist the ends to seal.

Refrigerate until firm.

Lemon-Basil Butter

This butter is perfect for adding a fresh and zesty flavor to your dishes. It's made with fresh lemon juice and basil, which add a delicious and tangy flavor to your meal.

Ingredients:

- 1 stick unsalted butter, room temperature
- 1 lemon, zested and juiced
- 1 tablespoon fresh basil, chopped
- Salt and pepper to taste

Instructions:

In a small bowl, combine the butter, lemon zest, lemon juice, and basil.
Mix well until all ingredients are fully incorporated.
Season with salt and pepper to taste.
Transfer the butter to a piece of parchment paper and shape into a log.
Wrap the parchment paper around the butter and twist the ends to seal.
Refrigerate until firm.

Sun-Dried Tomato Spread

This spread is perfect for adding a rich and savory flavor to your bread or crackers. It's made with sun-dried tomatoes and herbs, which add a delicious and robust flavor to your dish.

Ingredients:

- 1 cup sun-dried tomatoes, chopped
- 1/2 cup cream cheese, room temperature
- 1/4 cup mayonnaise
- 1 tablespoon fresh basil, chopped
- 1 garlic clove, minced
- Salt and pepper to taste

Instructions:

In a food processor, combine the sun-dried tomatoes, cream cheese, mayonnaise, basil, and garlic.
Pulse until all ingredients are fully incorporated and the mixture is smooth.
Season with salt and pepper to taste.
Transfer the spread to a bowl and refrigerate until ready to use.
Tips for Making Herb-Infused Butters and Spreads
Use fresh herbs: Fresh herbs have more flavor and nutrition than dried herbs, so it's always best to use fresh herbs when making herb-infused butters and spreads.
Experiment with different herbs and flavors: Feel free to experiment with different herbs and flavors to create your perfect butter or spread. You can also add in other ingredients, such as roasted garlic or roasted red peppers, to add even more flavor to your dish.
Customize to your taste: Adjust the amount of each ingredient to your taste preferences. If you prefer a stronger flavor, add more herbs. If you prefer a milder flavor, use less herbs.

Store in the fridge: Herb-infused butters and spreads can be stored in the fridge for up to a week. Just make sure to store them in an a sealed container or wrapped in parchment paper to prevent them from picking up any odors or flavors from other foods in the fridge.
Freeze for later use: If you don't plan on using your herb-infused butter or spread within a week, you can freeze it for later use. Simply wrap it tightly in plastic wrap and store it in the freezer for up to a month.
Use high-quality ingredients: When making herb-infused butters and spreads, it's important to use high-quality ingredients. This includes using unsalted butter, fresh herbs, and fresh garlic or other ingredients.
Don't overdo it with the herbs: While it's tempting to add lots of herbs to your butter or spread, it's important not to overdo it. Too many herbs can overpower the flavor of your dish and make it difficult to taste the other ingredients.
In conclusion, herb-infused butters and spreads are a delicious and easy way to add flavor and nutrition to your meals. Whether you prefer a classic garlic-herb butter or a zesty lemon-basil butter, there are endless possibilities for creating delicious and unique herb-infused butters and spreads. By using fresh herbs and high-quality ingredients, experimenting with different flavors, and customizing to your taste, you can create a butter or spread that perfectly complements any dish.

27. Making the Perfect Herb-infused Cheese

Cheese is a versatile ingredient that can be used in a variety of dishes, from appetizers to main courses to desserts. By adding herbs to cheese, you can elevate its flavor profile and create a unique and delicious dish. In this chapter, we will discuss how to make the perfect herb-infused cheese, including the best herbs to use, techniques for infusing the cheese, and tips for serving and storing.

Choosing the Right Herbs

When choosing herbs to infuse into cheese, it's important to select herbs that complement the flavor of the cheese. For example, soft, mild cheeses like brie or camembert pair well with delicate herbs like chives, tarragon, or thyme. Hard, aged cheeses like cheddar or parmesan can handle stronger herbs like rosemary, sage, or oregano.

Here are some popular herbs to consider for your herb-infused cheese:

- Basil
- Chives
- Cilantro
- Dill
- Garlic
- Oregano
- Rosemary
- Sage
- Thyme

While fresh herbs are preferred for their vibrant flavor, dried herbs can also be used if fresh ones are not available. Keep in mind that dried herbs have a more concentrated flavor, so use them sparingly.

Infusing the Cheese

There are several methods for infusing cheese with herbs, including mixing the herbs directly into the cheese, coating the cheese in herbs, and creating a herb-infused oil or butter to brush onto the cheese.

Method 1: Mixing Herbs Directly into the Cheese

One of the easiest ways to infuse cheese with herbs is to simply mix the herbs directly into the cheese. Start by softening the cheese at room temperature, then mix in finely chopped fresh herbs or dried herbs. Use a fork or spatula to blend the herbs evenly throughout the cheese. You can also add other ingredients like minced garlic or lemon zest to further enhance the flavor.

Method 2: Coating Cheese in Herbs

Another method for infusing cheese with herbs is to coat the cheese in a mixture of herbs and other flavorful ingredients. Start by preparing a mixture of finely chopped fresh herbs, minced garlic, and spices. Roll the cheese in the herb mixture, pressing the herbs gently into the surface of the cheese. The herbs will adhere to the cheese, creating a flavorful crust. This method works well with soft cheeses like goat cheese or cream cheese.

Method 3: Creating a Herb-infused Oil or Butter

A third method for infusing cheese with herbs is to create a herb-infused oil or butter to brush onto the cheese. Start by heating oil or butter in a small saucepan over low heat, then add fresh herbs and garlic. Allow the herbs and garlic to infuse the oil or butter for several minutes, then strain out the solids. Brush the herb-infused oil or butter onto the cheese, then allow it to sit at room temperature for 30 minutes to allow the flavors to meld.

Tips for Serving and Storing Herb-infused Cheese

Once you've created your perfect herb-infused cheese, here are some tips for serving and storing it:

Let the cheese come to room temperature: Before serving herb-infused cheese, allow it to come to room temperature. This will help to bring out the flavors and aromas of the herbs.

Pair the cheese with complementary ingredients: Herb-infused cheese pairs well with a variety of ingredients, including crackers, bread, nuts, and fruits. Consider serving it alongside a fruit and nut platter or a charcuterie board.

Store the cheese properly: Herb-infused cheese should be stored in the refrigerator in an airtight container. It's best to consume the cheese within a few days.

Label the cheese: It's a good idea to label your herb-infused cheese with the type of cheese and the herbs used in the infusion. This will help you keep track of what flavors you've used and make it easier to recreate your favorite combinations.

Experiment with different combinations: Don't be afraid to experiment with different herb and cheese combinations to find your favorite flavors. Try mixing different herbs together or using a blend of dried and fresh herbs for a more complex flavor.

Herb-infused Cheese Recipes

Here are two simple recipes to get you started with herb-infused cheese:

Herb-infused Goat Cheese

Ingredients:

- 4 ounces goat cheese
- 1 tablespoon finely chopped fresh herbs (such as chives, thyme, and tarragon)
- 1 garlic clove, minced
- Salt and pepper to taste

Instructions:

Soften the goat cheese at room temperature.

In a small bowl, mix together the herbs, garlic, salt, and pepper.

Using a fork or spatula, mix the herb mixture into the goat cheese until evenly blended.

Serve at room temperature with crackers or bread.

Herb-infused Parmesan Cheese

Ingredients:

- 1 cup grated parmesan cheese
- 2 tablespoons olive oil
- 2 garlic cloves, minced
- 1 tablespoon finely chopped fresh herbs (such as rosemary and oregano)
- Salt and pepper to taste

Instructions:

In a small saucepan, heat the olive oil and garlic over low heat for 2-3 minutes until fragrant.

Add the fresh herbs to the oil and heat for an additional minute.

Strain the oil through a fine-mesh sieve to remove the herbs and garlic solids.

In a small bowl, mix together the grated parmesan cheese, herb-infused oil, salt, and pepper.

Roll the cheese mixture into small balls or shape it into a log.

Chill the cheese in the refrigerator for 30 minutes before serving.

In conclusion, herb-infused cheese is a simple and delicious way to add a new dimension of flavor to your cheese dishes. With a little experimentation, you can create a variety of unique and delicious combinations that will impress your family and friends. Whether you're serving it as an appetizer, topping a salad, or using it in a main dish, herb-infused cheese is sure to add a burst of flavor to any dish.

28. Herb-infused Breads and Rolls

Bread is a staple food that has been a part of human diets for thousands of years. It is an incredibly versatile food that can be made in a variety of ways, with a wide range of flavors and ingredients. One way to add flavor to your bread is by using herbs. Herb-infused breads and rolls are not only delicious, but also add a healthy boost of nutrients to your diet. In this chapter, we will explore different herbs and techniques for infusing bread with their unique flavors.

Choosing the Right Herbs

When it comes to herb-infused breads and rolls, the possibilities are endless. However, some herbs are better suited for baking than others. Here are a few herbs that are commonly used in breads and rolls:

Rosemary: This woody herb has a distinct and strong flavor that pairs well with bread. It is often used in savory breads and rolls, such as focaccia and ciabatta.

Thyme: With its delicate and subtle flavor, thyme is a great choice for breads and rolls that need a mild herbaceous flavor. It pairs well with butter and cheese, making it a great addition to dinner rolls.

Sage: This herb has a slightly bitter taste and is often used in stuffing, but it also works well in breads and rolls. It pairs well with cheese and makes a great addition to savory breads.

Basil: This herb has a sweet and mild flavor that pairs well with tomatoes and cheese. It is often used in focaccia and other Italian-style breads.

Dill: This herb has a fresh and delicate flavor that pairs well with fish and seafood. It is often used in dill bread, which is a popular Scandinavian bread.

Techniques for Infusing Herbs in Bread

There are several techniques for infusing herbs into bread dough. Here are a few methods to try:

Adding dried herbs to the dough: This is the simplest method for infusing herbs into bread. Simply add the dried herbs to the flour before mixing in the other ingredients. You can adjust the amount of herbs to your liking.

Infusing herbs into the liquid: This method involves steeping fresh or dried herbs in the liquid used in the dough. This can be done by adding the herbs to warm milk, water or oil and letting it sit for 10-15 minutes. Then strain out the herbs before using the liquid in the dough.

Mixing fresh herbs into the dough: Fresh herbs can be finely chopped and mixed into the dough just before shaping. This method works well with soft herbs such as basil or parsley.

Topping the bread with fresh herbs: Another way to add herbs to your bread is by topping the bread dough with fresh herbs just before baking. This works particularly well with rosemary and thyme.

Herb-Infused Bread Recipes

Here are two recipes for herb-infused breads that are easy to make and delicious:

Rosemary Focaccia

Ingredients:

- 4 cups all-purpose flour
- 2 teaspoons instant yeast
- 1 teaspoon salt
- 1/4 cup olive oil
- 1 1/2 cups warm water
- 1 tablespoon fresh rosemary leaves, finely chopped
- Sea salt, for topping

Instructions:

In a large mixing bowl, whisk together the flour, yeast, and salt.

Add the olive oil and warm water to the dry ingredients and stir until the dough comes together.

Knead the dough for 5-7 minutes until smooth and elastic.

Cover the dough and let it rest for 1 hour in a warm place.

Preheat the oven to 400°F.

Punch down the dough and transfer it to a lightly greased baking sheet.

Use your fingers to press the dough into a rectangle shape, about 1 inch thick.

Sprinkle the rosemary leaves over the top of the dough and press them in slightly.

Sprinkle sea salt over the top of the dough.

Bake for 20-25 minutes, until the bread is golden brown and sounds hollow when tapped.

Let cool for 10 minutes before slicing and serving.

Dill Bread

Ingredients:

- 3 cups all-purpose flour
- 1 tablespoon sugar
- 1 tablespoon instant yeast
- 1 teaspoon salt
- 1/2 cup warm milk
- 1/2 cup warm water
- 2 tablespoons unsalted butter, melted
- 1/4 cup chopped fresh dill

Instructions:

In a large mixing bowl, whisk together the flour, sugar, yeast, and salt.

Add the warm milk, warm water, and melted butter to the dry ingredients and stir until the dough comes together.

Knead the dough for 5-7 minutes until smooth and elastic.

Cover the dough and let it rest for 1 hour in a warm place.

Preheat the oven to 375°F.

Punch down the dough and transfer it to a lightly greased loaf pan.

Press the chopped dill into the top of the dough.

Bake for 30-35 minutes, until the bread is golden brown and sounds hollow when tapped.

Let cool for 10 minutes before slicing and serving.

In conclusion, herb-infused breads and rolls are a delicious and healthy way to add flavor to your diet. With the right herbs and techniques, you can create a variety of breads with unique and delicious flavors. Experiment with different herbs and methods to find your favorite combinations. Whether you are making focaccia, ciabatta, dinner rolls or sandwich bread, adding herbs will take your bread to the next level.

29. Herb-infused Pasta and Noodle Dishes

Pasta and noodles are a staple in many cuisines around the world. They are versatile, filling and easy to prepare. Adding herbs to pasta and noodle dishes not only enhances their flavor but also adds health benefits. Herbs such as basil, parsley, thyme, and oregano contain antioxidants, vitamins, and minerals that can improve digestion, boost the immune system, and reduce inflammation. In this chapter, we will explore different ways to incorporate herbs into pasta and noodle dishes.

Herb-infused Pasta

Herb-infused pasta is a simple and delicious way to add flavor to your dishes. There are different ways to make herb-infused pasta. One way is to mix chopped herbs into the pasta dough before rolling it out. Another way is to add herbs to the pasta water. Here are two recipes for herb-infused pasta:

Basil Pasta

Ingredients:

- 2 cups all-purpose flour
- 1/4 teaspoon salt
- 2 tablespoons chopped fresh basil
- 2 eggs
- 1 tablespoon olive oil
- 1-2 tablespoons water (as needed)

Instructions:

In a large mixing bowl, whisk together the flour, salt, and chopped basil.
Add the eggs and olive oil to the bowl and mix until the dough comes together.
Knead the dough for 5-7 minutes until smooth and elastic.
Cover the dough and let it rest for 30 minutes in a cool place.
Roll out the dough to the desired thickness.
Cut the pasta into the desired shape, such as fettuccine or spaghetti.
Cook the pasta in boiling water for 2-3 minutes or until al dente.
Drain the pasta and toss it with your favorite sauce.

Thyme Pasta

Ingredients:

- 2 cups all-purpose flour

- 1/4 teaspoon salt
- 2 tablespoons chopped fresh thyme
- 2 eggs
- 1 tablespoon olive oil
- 1-2 tablespoons water (as needed)

Instructions:

In a large mixing bowl, whisk together the flour, salt, and chopped thyme.
Add the eggs and olive oil to the bowl and mix until the dough comes together.
Knead the dough for 5-7 minutes until smooth and elastic.
Cover the dough and let it rest for 30 minutes in a cool place.
Roll out the dough to the desired thickness.
Cut the pasta into the desired shape, such as fusilli or penne.
Add the pasta to boiling water with a handful of fresh thyme leaves.
Cook the pasta for 2-3 minutes or until al dente.
Drain the pasta and toss it with olive oil, garlic, and Parmesan cheese.

Herb-infused Noodle Dishes

Noodle dishes are popular in Asian cuisine and can be prepared in many different ways. Adding herbs to noodle dishes can enhance their flavor and provide health benefits. Here are two recipes for herb-infused noodle dishes:

Ginger and Cilantro Noodles

Ingredients:

- 8 oz. noodles, such as udon or soba
- 2 tablespoons sesame oil
- 2 tablespoons soy sauce
- 1 tablespoon rice vinegar
- 1 tablespoon honey
- 1 tablespoon grated fresh ginger
- 1/4 cup chopped fresh cilantro

Instructions:

Cook the noodles according to the package directions.
In a small mixing bowl, whisk together the sesame oil, soy sauce, rice vinegar, honey, and grated ginger.
Drain the noodles and toss them with the sauce.
Sprinkle the chopped cilantro over the noodles and toss to combine.
5. Serve the ginger and cilantro noodles warm or cold.

Lemon and Basil Noodles

Ingredients:

- 8 oz. noodles, such as spaghetti or linguine
- 2 tablespoons olive oil
- Zest and juice of 1 lemon
- 2 tablespoons chopped fresh basil
- 1/4 teaspoon red pepper flakes (optional)
- Salt and pepper to taste

Instructions:

Cook the noodles according to the package directions.

In a small bowl, whisk together the olive oil, lemon zest, lemon juice, chopped basil, red pepper flakes (if using), salt, and pepper.

Drain the noodles and toss them with the lemon and basil mixture.

Serve the lemon and basil noodles warm or cold.

In conclusion, herb-infused pasta and noodle dishes are a delightful way to incorporate the flavors and health benefits of herbs into your meals. Whether you choose to infuse the pasta itself or add herbs to the sauce or dressing, the result will be a dish bursting with freshness and flavor. Experiment with different herb combinations and types of pasta to discover your favorite combinations. By incorporating herbs into your pasta and noodle dishes, you'll not only elevate their taste but also enjoy the added nutritional benefits that herbs bring to the table.

30. Herb-infused Rice and Grain Recipes

Herbs are an essential ingredient in cooking, and they add not only flavor but also nutritional value to dishes. Herb-infused rice and grain dishes are a delicious and easy way to incorporate the benefits of herbs into your diet. In this chapter, we will explore some of the best herb-infused rice and grain recipes that will enhance your meals and provide a healthy boost.

Herb-Infused Rice Pilaf

Ingredients:

- 1 cup long-grain white rice
- 1 3/4 cups chicken or vegetable broth
- 2 tablespoons unsalted butter
- 2 tablespoons olive oil
- 1 medium onion, chopped
- 2 garlic cloves, minced
- 1/4 cup chopped fresh parsley
- 1/4 cup chopped fresh cilantro
- 1/4 cup chopped fresh dill
- Salt and black pepper, to taste

Instructions:

In a medium saucepan, combine the rice, broth, and a pinch of salt. Bring to a boil, then reduce heat to low and cover the saucepan with a lid.

Cook for 18-20 minutes, or until the liquid has been absorbed and the rice is tender.

In a large skillet, melt the butter with the olive oil over medium heat. Add the onion and garlic and sauté until the onion is translucent, about 5-7 minutes.

Add the cooked rice to the skillet and stir until well combined with the onion and garlic mixture.

Add the chopped parsley, cilantro, dill, salt, and black pepper. Stir well and cook for another 2-3 minutes until the herbs are fragrant.

Serve the herb-infused rice pilaf as a side dish to your favorite meat or vegetable dish.

Herb-Infused Quinoa Salad

Ingredients:

- 1 cup quinoa
- 2 cups water
- 1/2 cup chopped fresh parsley
- 1/2 cup chopped fresh mint
- 1/2 cup chopped fresh cilantro
- 1/4 cup chopped green onions
- 1/4 cup chopped red onion
- 1/4 cup extra-virgin olive oil
- 3 tablespoons fresh lemon juice
- Salt and black pepper, to taste

Instructions:

Rinse the quinoa thoroughly in a fine-mesh strainer.

In a medium saucepan, combine the quinoa and water. Bring to a boil, then reduce heat to low and cover the saucepan with a lid.

Cook for 15-20 minutes, or until the water has been absorbed and the quinoa is tender.

In a large bowl, combine the cooked quinoa, chopped parsley, mint, cilantro, green onions, and red onion.

In a small bowl, whisk together the olive oil, lemon juice, salt, and black pepper.

Pour the dressing over the quinoa mixture and toss until well combined.

Serve the herb-infused quinoa salad at room temperature or chilled.

Herb-Infused Brown Rice Bowl

Ingredients:

- 1 cup brown rice
- 2 cups water
- 2 tablespoons olive oil
- 1 red bell pepper, diced
- 1 yellow bell pepper, diced
- 1 zucchini, diced
- 2 garlic cloves, minced
- 1 teaspoon dried basil
- 1 teaspoon dried oregano
- Salt and black pepper, to taste
- 1/4 cup chopped fresh parsley
- 1/4 cup chopped fresh cilantro

Instructions:

Rinse the brown rice thoroughly in a fine-mesh strainer.

In a medium saucepan, combine the rice and water. Bring to a boil, then reduce heat to low and cover the saucepan with a lid.

Cook for 40-45 minutes, or until the water has been absorbed and the rice is tender.

In a large skillet, heat the olive oil over medium heat. Add the diced red and yellow bell peppers, zucchini, and minced garlic. Sauté for 5-7 minutes, or until the vegetables are tender.

Stir in the dried basil, dried oregano, salt, and black pepper. Cook for an additional 2-3 minutes to allow the flavors to blend.

Add the cooked brown rice to the skillet with the sautéed vegetables. Stir well to combine and heat through.

Remove from heat and sprinkle the chopped parsley and cilantro over the rice bowl. Toss lightly to distribute the herbs evenly.

Serve the herb-infused brown rice bowl as a wholesome and flavorful main dish or as a side to complement grilled meats or roasted vegetables.

Herb-Infused Couscous with Roasted Vegetables

Ingredients:

- 1 cup couscous
- 1 1/4 cups vegetable broth
- 2 tablespoons olive oil
- 1 small eggplant, diced
- 1 red bell pepper, diced
- 1 yellow bell pepper, diced
- 1 small red onion, thinly sliced
- 2 cloves garlic, minced
- 1 teaspoon dried thyme
- 1 teaspoon dried rosemary
- Salt and black pepper, to taste
- 1/4 cup chopped fresh basil
- 1/4 cup chopped fresh mint

Instructions:

Preheat the oven to 400°F (200°C).

Place the diced eggplant, red and yellow bell peppers, and sliced red onion on a baking sheet. Drizzle with olive oil and sprinkle with minced garlic, dried thyme, dried rosemary, salt, and black pepper. Toss to coat the vegetables evenly.

Roast the vegetables in the preheated oven for 25-30 minutes, or until they are tender and lightly browned.

While the vegetables are roasting, prepare the couscous. In a saucepan, bring the vegetable broth to a boil. Remove from heat and stir in the couscous. Cover the saucepan with a lid and let it sit for 5 minutes.

Fluff the couscous with a fork and transfer it to a large bowl.

Add the roasted vegetables to the bowl with the couscous. Toss gently to combine.

Sprinkle the chopped fresh basil and mint over the couscous mixture. Toss again to distribute the herbs throughout the dish.

Serve the herb-infused couscous with roasted vegetables as a satisfying vegetarian main course or as a flavorful side dish.

In conclusion, herb-infused rice and grain recipes offer a delightful way to incorporate the flavors and health benefits of herbs into your meals. Whether it's a fragrant rice pilaf, a refreshing quinoa salad, a nourishing brown rice bowl, or a flavorful couscous dish, herbs bring a new dimension to these dishes. Experiment with different herbs, such as parsley, cilantro, basil, thyme, and rosemary, to create your unique combinations. By incorporating herb-infused rice and grain recipes into your cooking repertoire, you'll not only elevate the taste of your dishes but also enjoy the nutritional benefits that herbs bring to the table.

31. Making the Perfect Herb-infused Soup Stocks

Soup stocks form the foundation of many delicious soups, stews, and sauces. Infusing stocks with herbs can enhance the flavor profile and add depth and complexity to your dishes. In this chapter, we will discuss the basics of making the perfect herb-infused soup stocks.

Soup Stocks

Ingredients:

- Bones or vegetables
- Water
- Onion
- Carrots
- Celery
- Garlic
- Fresh herbs such as thyme, bay leaves, parsley, and rosemary
- Salt and pepper

Steps to Making the Perfect Herb-Infused Soup Stocks:

Start with the right ingredients:

For meat-based stocks, use bones such as chicken, beef, pork, or lamb.

For vegetable-based stocks, use a mix of vegetables such as onions, carrots, celery, and garlic.

Use high-quality ingredients, as the quality of the stock will depend on the ingredients used.

Roast the ingredients (optional):

Roasting the ingredients can add depth and complexity to the stock. Roasting bones, vegetables, and herbs in the oven for 20-30 minutes at 400°F will add a rich, caramelized flavor to the stock.

Add water:

Cover the bones or vegetables with cold water in a large pot.

Use a ratio of 2:1 water to bones/vegetables.

Bring the water to a boil, then reduce the heat to a low simmer.

Skim the surface:

As the stock simmers, impurities will rise to the surface. Skim the surface with a spoon or skimmer to remove any foam or impurities.
Add aromatics:
Add a mix of aromatics such as onions, carrots, celery, and garlic to the pot.
Use a ratio of 1 onion, 2 carrots, 2 celery stalks, and 2-3 garlic cloves per 2-3 pounds of bones/vegetables.
For herb-infused stocks, add fresh herbs such as thyme, bay leaves, parsley, and rosemary.
Simmer for several hours:
The longer the stock simmers, the more flavorful it will be. Simmer meat-based stocks for at least 4-6 hours and vegetable-based stocks for 2-3 hours.
During the simmering process, check the stock occasionally and add more water as needed to keep the bones/vegetables covered.
Strain the stock:
Once the stock has simmered, strain it through a fine-mesh strainer or cheesecloth to remove any solids.
Discard the solids and reserve the liquid.
Add salt and pepper:
Taste the stock and add salt and pepper as needed.
Cool and store:
Allow the stock to cool to room temperature, then refrigerate or freeze it.
Use the stock within 3-4 days if refrigerated or up to 6 months if frozen.
Tips for Making the Perfect Herb-Infused Soup Stocks:
Use fresh herbs:
Fresh herbs will add more flavor to the stock than dried herbs.
Add the herbs in the last hour of simmering to avoid overpowering the stock.
Experiment with different herbs:
Try different herb combinations to find your favorite flavor profile.
Some good herb combinations include thyme and rosemary, parsley and bay leaves, and cilantro and ginger.
Use high-quality ingredients:
The quality of the ingredients used will determine the quality of the stock.
Use organic, grass-fed, or pasture-raised bones and fresh, organic vegetables for the best results.
Don't add too much salt:

It's best to add salt and pepper to the cooled stock after straining and tasting it. This allows you to control the seasoning and prevents the stock from becoming overly salty.

Label and date your stock:

When storing the stock, be sure to label the container with the type of stock and the date it was made. This helps you keep track of your stocks and ensures you use them within a reasonable time frame.

Freeze stock in smaller portions:

Consider freezing the stock in smaller portions, such as in ice cube trays or small freezer bags. This allows for easy portioning and thawing when you only need a small amount for a recipe.

Herb-Infused Stock Variations:

Classic Herb Stock

For a versatile herb-infused stock, add a combination of fresh herbs such as thyme, parsley, and bay leaves. These herbs provide a well-rounded flavor that complements a wide range of soups and dishes.

Asian-Inspired Stock

Infuse the stock with herbs and spices commonly used in Asian cuisine, such as lemongrass, ginger, and star anise. This aromatic stock is perfect for making Asian-inspired soups, like pho or ramen.

Mediterranean Herb Stock

Create a Mediterranean flair by infusing the stock with herbs like rosemary, oregano, and basil. This aromatic and flavorful stock is excellent for adding depth to Mediterranean-style soups, stews, and sauces.

Herb and Mushroom Stock

Enhance the earthy flavors of the stock by adding a combination of herbs and dried mushrooms, such as porcini or shiitake. This stock adds a rich umami taste, perfect for vegetarian and vegan recipes.

Herb-Infused Vegetable Stock

For a vegetable-based stock, infuse it with a variety of fresh herbs such as thyme, parsley, and basil, along with vegetables like onions, carrots, and celery. This stock provides a robust flavor base for vegetarian soups and stews.

In conclusion, mastering the art of making herb-infused soup stocks is a valuable skill that will elevate your culinary creations. By using high-quality ingredients and infusing the stock with a carefully selected combination of herbs, you can enhance the flavor profile and nutritional value of your dishes. Experiment with different herb combinations and variations to create stocks that suit your taste preferences and complement the recipes you love. With homemade herb-infused stocks, you'll be able to add depth and complexity to soups, stews, sauces, and more, taking your cooking to new heights of flavor and health.

32. Herb-infused Broths and Bouillons

Herb-infused broths and bouillons are an essential component of many culinary dishes. They add depth, richness, and complexity to a wide range of recipes, from soups and stews to sauces and gravies. By infusing the broth with a carefully selected combination of herbs, you can enhance the flavor profile and nutritional value of your dishes. In this chapter, we will explore the art of making herb-infused broths and bouillons, including various herb combinations and variations to suit your taste preferences and complement your favorite recipes.

The Importance of Quality Ingredients

The key to making a flavorful and nutritious broth or bouillon is to start with high-quality ingredients. Using fresh vegetables, herbs, and spices will yield the best results. For a vegetable-based broth, use a combination of onions, carrots, celery, and garlic. For a meat-based broth, use high-quality cuts of meat, such as chicken or beef bones.

Choosing the Right Herbs

Herbs play a crucial role in infusing the broth with flavor and aroma. When selecting herbs, it's important to consider the flavor profile and nutritional benefits. Here are some common herbs and their flavor profiles:

Thyme: Thyme adds a slightly sweet and earthy flavor to the broth. It's also a good source of vitamin C and is believed to have antibacterial properties.

Rosemary: Rosemary adds a distinctive, pine-like flavor to the broth. It's also rich in antioxidants and has anti-inflammatory properties.

Sage: Sage adds a slightly bitter and peppery flavor to the broth. It's also believed to have antimicrobial properties and may help improve brain function.

Parsley: Parsley adds a fresh and slightly sweet flavor to the broth. It's also a good source of vitamin K and has anti-inflammatory properties.

Bay leaves: Bay leaves add a subtle, sweet, and slightly floral flavor to the broth. They're also believed to have anti-inflammatory properties and may help improve digestion.

Infusing the Broth with Herbs

There are several ways to infuse the broth with herbs. Here are some methods:

Simmering: Simmering the herbs in the broth for an extended period allows the flavors to infuse. Tie the herbs together with twine or place them in a cheesecloth sachet to make them easy to remove.
Steeping: Steeping the herbs in hot water for a few minutes and then adding the herb-infused water to the broth allows for a more delicate infusion of flavor.
Blending: Blend the herbs with a small amount of the broth and then add the mixture to the rest of the broth. This method allows for a more concentrated infusion of flavor.
Herb-Infused Broth and Bouillon Variations:

Classic Herb Broth

For a versatile herb-infused broth, add a combination of fresh herbs such as thyme, parsley, and bay leaves. These herbs provide a well-rounded flavor that complements a wide range of soups and dishes.

Asian-Inspired Broth

Infuse the broth with herbs and spices commonly used in Asian cuisine, such as lemongrass, ginger, and star anise. This aromatic broth is perfect for making Asian-inspired soups, like pho or ramen.

Mediterranean Herb Broth

Create a Mediterranean flair by infusing the broth with herbs like rosemary, oregano, and basil. This aromatic and flavorful broth is excellent for adding depth to Mediterranean-style soups, stews, and sauces.

Herb and Mushroom Broth

Enhance the earthy flavors of the broth by adding a combination of herbs and dried mushrooms, such as porcini or shiitake. This broth adds a rich umami taste, perfect for vegetarian and vegan recipes.

Healing Herb Broth

Infuse the broth with healing herbs such as turmeric, ginger, and garlic. These herbs are known for their anti-inflammatory and immune-boosting properties, making this broth an excellent choice for nourishing and comforting soups.

Herb Bouillon Cubes

Make your own herb-infused bouillon cubes for quick and convenient flavoring. Simply blend a combination of herbs, salt, and spices, and then freeze the mixture in an ice cube tray. These cubes can be added to soups, stews, and sauces to enhance the flavor instantly.
Using Herb-Infused Broths and Bouillons:

Soups and Stews

Use herb-infused broths as the base for a variety of soups and stews. The infused flavors will elevate the overall taste and provide a depth of flavor that enhances the entire dish.

Sauces and Gravies

Add herb-infused broths or bouillons to sauces and gravies to enhance the flavor and create a rich, aromatic base. The herbs will add complexity to the sauce, making it more flavorful and enjoyable.

Poaching and Braising

When poaching or braising meats or vegetables, use herb-infused broths as the cooking liquid. This will infuse the ingredients with the flavors of the herbs, resulting in a deliciously seasoned and tender dish.

Rice and Grain Dishes

Use herb-infused broths instead of water when cooking rice or grains. This simple swap adds an extra layer of flavor and elevates the entire dish.

Flavorful Cooking Liquid

Use herb-infused broths as a flavorful cooking liquid for steaming vegetables or cooking pasta. The herbs will impart their aromatic qualities to the ingredients, enhancing their natural flavors.

In conclusion, herb-infused broths and bouillons are versatile and essential components of many culinary dishes. By infusing broths with carefully selected herbs, you can elevate the flavor profile and nutritional value of your recipes. Experiment with different herb combinations and variations to create broths and bouillons that suit your taste preferences and complement your favorite dishes. With homemade herb-infused broths and bouillons, you can enhance the taste and health benefits of your soups, stews, sauces, and more, taking your culinary creations to new heights. Embrace the power of herbs and let them transform your cooking into a flavorful and satisfying experience.

33. Herb-infused Creams and Sauces

Herbs can add a burst of flavor and aroma to any dish. When combined with creams and sauces, they can transform a simple meal into a gourmet delight. Whether you are looking to enhance the taste of your pasta, chicken, or seafood, herb-infused creams and sauces are a perfect choice. In this chapter, we will explore some simple yet delicious herb-infused creams and sauces that you can easily prepare at home.

Herb-infused Creams

Basil Cream: This creamy sauce is perfect for pasta, chicken, or seafood. To make basil cream, heat 1 cup of heavy cream in a saucepan over medium heat until it begins to simmer. Add 1/4 cup of chopped fresh basil and simmer for an additional 5 minutes. Remove from heat and let the sauce cool for a few minutes. Then, pour the sauce into a blender and blend until smooth. Season with salt and pepper to taste.

Tarragon Cream: Tarragon adds a unique flavor to this creamy sauce, which pairs perfectly with chicken or fish. To make tarragon cream, heat 1 cup of heavy cream in a saucepan over medium heat until it begins to simmer. Add 1/4 cup of chopped fresh tarragon and simmer for an additional 5 minutes. Remove from heat and let the sauce cool for a few minutes. Then, pour the sauce into a blender and blend until smooth. Season with salt and pepper to taste.

Rosemary Cream: This creamy sauce is perfect for lamb, chicken, or potatoes. To make rosemary cream, heat 1 cup of heavy cream in a saucepan over medium heat until it begins to simmer. Add 1/4 cup of chopped fresh rosemary and simmer for an additional 5 minutes. Remove from heat and let the sauce cool for a few minutes. Then, pour the sauce into a blender and blend until smooth. Season with salt and pepper to taste.

Herb-infused Sauces

Lemon and Thyme Sauce: This tangy sauce is perfect for chicken, fish, or vegetables. To make lemon and thyme sauce, melt 2 tablespoons of butter in a saucepan over medium heat. Add 2 tablespoons of chopped fresh thyme and cook for 1 minute. Add 1/4 cup of fresh lemon juice and 1/4 cup of chicken broth. Bring to a boil and simmer for 5 minutes. Remove from heat and let the sauce cool for a few minutes. Then, pour the sauce into a blender and blend until smooth. Season with salt and pepper to taste.

Garlic and Chive Sauce: This savory sauce is perfect for steak, chicken, or potatoes. To make garlic and chive sauce, melt 2 tablespoons of butter in a saucepan over medium heat. Add 2 cloves of minced garlic and cook for 1 minute. Add 1/4 cup of chopped fresh chives and cook for an additional minute. Add 1/4 cup of heavy cream and bring to a simmer. Simmer for 5 minutes, then remove from heat and let the sauce cool for a few minutes. Then, pour the sauce into a blender and blend until smooth. Season with salt and pepper to taste.

Cilantro Lime Sauce: This zesty sauce is perfect for fish, chicken, or tacos. To make cilantro lime sauce, blend 1/2 cup of fresh cilantro, 1/4 cup of fresh lime juice, 1/4 cup of olive oil, and 1 clove of garlic in a blender until smooth. Season with salt and pepper to taste.

Tips for Making Herb-infused Creams and Sauces

Use fresh ingredients: For the best flavor, always use fresh herbs in your herb-infused creams and sauces. Fresh herbs have a vibrant taste and aroma that can elevate your dish to another level. If fresh herbs are not available, you can use dried herbs, but keep in mind that the flavor might be slightly different.

Infuse the flavors: To infuse the flavors of the herbs into your creams and sauces, it's important to heat them gently. This allows the herbs to release their oils and flavors into the cream or sauce. Simmer the herbs in the cream or sauce for a few minutes to achieve the desired infusion. Avoid boiling the mixture as it can cause the cream or sauce to curdle.

Strain the mixture: After simmering the herbs in the cream or sauce, it's a good idea to strain the mixture to remove any herb remnants. This ensures a smooth and consistent texture in your final sauce.

Use a blender or food processor: To achieve a creamy and smooth consistency in your herb-infused creams and sauces, it's recommended to use a blender or food processor. This will help break down the herbs and blend them seamlessly into the cream or sauce. Blend the mixture until you reach the desired consistency.

Season to taste: Always taste and season your herb-infused creams and sauces before serving. Adjust the salt, pepper, and other seasonings according to your preference. Remember that herbs can vary in intensity, so start with a little seasoning and add more if needed.

Pairing with dishes: Herb-infused creams and sauces can be incredibly versatile and complement a wide range of dishes. Consider the flavor profiles of your sauces and match them with appropriate dishes. For example, basil cream goes well with pasta dishes, while tarragon cream pairs beautifully with chicken or fish. Experiment with different combinations to find your favorite pairings.

Storing leftovers: If you have any leftover herb-infused creams and sauces, store them in airtight containers in the refrigerator. They can usually be kept for a few days, but it's best to consume them as soon as possible for optimal flavor.

In conclusion, herb-infused creams and sauces are a fantastic way to add depth, flavor, and freshness to your culinary creations. By infusing creams and sauces with carefully selected herbs, you can elevate simple dishes to gourmet experiences. Experiment with different herb combinations and variations to create your signature sauces that suit your taste preferences and complement your favorite recipes. With homemade herb-infused creams and sauces, you can bring a burst of flavor and a touch of elegance to any meal. Embrace the versatility of herbs and let them inspire your culinary creativity.

34. Herb-infused Dressings and Marinades

Dressings and marinades are essential components of many dishes. They add flavor, moisture, and depth to salads, meats, vegetables, and more. Using herbs in dressings and marinades can elevate the flavor profile of any dish. In this chapter, we will discuss the basics of making herb-infused dressings and marinades, the different types of herbs that work well in these preparations, and some delicious recipes to try at home.

The Basics of Making Herb-infused Dressings and Marinades

Making herb-infused dressings and marinades is a straightforward process. To infuse herbs into your dressing or marinade, you can either use fresh or dried herbs. Fresh herbs have a more potent flavor, while dried herbs have a more concentrated flavor. You can also use a combination of both for added complexity.

To make herb-infused dressings, simply combine your chosen herbs with a base of oil and vinegar or lemon juice. The ratio of oil to vinegar or lemon juice can vary depending on your preference. For a basic vinaigrette, a ratio of three parts oil to one part vinegar or lemon juice is a good starting point. To make your dressing creamier, you can add mayonnaise or sour cream.

To make herb-infused marinades, you will need a base of oil and acid, such as lemon juice or vinegar, and some additional flavorings like garlic, ginger, and soy sauce. Herbs can be added to the marinade to infuse the meat or vegetables with their flavor. Marinate your protein for at least 30 minutes, but up to 24 hours, depending on the cut and your desired level of flavor.

Types of Herbs to Use

There are many herbs that work well in dressings and marinades. Some of the most popular herbs include:

Basil: Basil adds a sweet, slightly minty flavor to dressings and marinades. It pairs well with tomato-based dishes, grilled meats, and seafood.

Cilantro: Cilantro has a bright, citrusy flavor and is often used in Mexican and Asian cuisine. It pairs well with grilled meats, vegetables, and seafood.

Dill: Dill has a slightly sweet, licorice-like flavor that pairs well with fish, potatoes, and cucumber-based dishes.

Rosemary: Rosemary has a strong, pine-like flavor that works well with roasted meats and vegetables.
Thyme: Thyme has a slightly sweet, earthy flavor that pairs well with roasted meats, vegetables, and potatoes.
Oregano: Oregano has a slightly bitter, pungent flavor that pairs well with tomato-based dishes, grilled meats, and vegetables.
Recipes

Classic Herb Vinaigrette

Ingredients:

- 1/2 cup olive oil
- 1/4 cup red wine vinegar
- 1 garlic clove, minced
- 1 tbsp Dijon mustard
- 1 tbsp chopped fresh basil
- 1 tbsp chopped fresh thyme
- Salt and pepper, to taste

Directions:

In a small bowl, whisk together the olive oil, red wine vinegar, garlic, Dijon mustard, and herbs.
Season with salt and pepper, to taste.
Store in an airtight container in the refrigerator for up to one week.

Lemon Herb Marinade

Ingredients:

- 1/2 cup olive oil
- 1/4 cup fresh lemon juice
- 2 garlic cloves, minced
- 1 tbsp chopped fresh rosemary
- 1 tbsp chopped fresh thyme
- Salt and pepper, to taste

Directions:

In a small bowl, whisk together the olive oil, lemon juice, minced garlic, and chopped herbs.
Season with salt and pepper, to taste.
Place your protein of choice, such as chicken, fish, or tofu, in a ziplock bag or a shallow dish.

Pour the marinade over the protein, making sure it is evenly coated.
Seal the bag or cover the dish and refrigerate for at least 30 minutes, or up to 24 hours for more intense flavor.
When ready to cook, remove the protein from the marinade and discard the marinade.
Cook the protein according to your preferred method, such as grilling, baking, or sautéing.

Greek Yogurt Herb Dressing

Ingredients:

- 1 cup plain Greek yogurt
- 2 tbsp fresh lemon juice
- 1 garlic clove, minced
- 2 tbsp chopped fresh dill
- 1 tbsp chopped fresh parsley
- 1 tbsp chopped fresh mint
- Salt and pepper, to taste

Directions:

In a medium bowl, whisk together the Greek yogurt, lemon juice, minced garlic, and chopped herbs.
Season with salt and pepper, to taste.
Adjust the consistency by adding a small amount of water if desired.
Use as a dressing for salads, as a dip for vegetables, or as a sauce for grilled meats.

Tips for Herb-infused Dressings and Marinades

Experiment with herb combinations: Don't be afraid to mix and match different herbs to create unique flavor profiles. Combining herbs like basil, parsley, and oregano can give your dressings and marinades a Mediterranean twist, while cilantro and lime can add a fresh and vibrant touch.
Adjust the intensity: The amount of herbs you use can vary depending on your personal taste preference. Start with smaller amounts and gradually increase until you reach the desired flavor intensity.
Let it rest: After preparing your herb-infused dressings and marinades, allow them to rest for at least 30 minutes before using. This resting period allows the flavors to meld together and develop.

Store properly: Store your dressings and marinades in airtight containers in the refrigerator. They can typically be kept for up to one week, but always check for any signs of spoilage before using.
Use as a finishing touch: Herb-infused dressings can also be used as a finishing touch to enhance the flavors of cooked dishes. Drizzle a spoonful over roasted vegetables or grilled meats to add a burst of freshness.
In conclusion, herb-infused dressings and marinades are a wonderful way to enhance the flavors of your dishes. By incorporating fresh or dried herbs into your dressings and marinades, you can create a myriad of flavors that complement a wide range of ingredients. Experiment with different herbs and flavor combinations to discover your favorite combinations. With herb-infused dressings and marinades, you can take your culinary creations to a new level of taste and freshness.

35. Herb-infused Dips and Spreads for Vegetables

Herbs are a great addition to any dip or spread for vegetables, adding not only flavor but also nutritional value. With so many different herbs to choose from, the possibilities for creating delicious and healthy dips and spreads are endless. In this chapter, we will explore some of the most popular herbs and how to use them to make herb-infused dips and spreads for vegetables.

Basil Dip

Basil is a flavorful herb that is often used in Italian cuisine. It has a sweet, slightly peppery flavor and pairs well with tomatoes, mozzarella, and other Italian ingredients. To make a basil dip, you will need:

Ingredients:

- 1 cup fresh basil leaves
- 1/2 cup mayonnaise
- 1/2 cup sour cream
- 1 garlic clove, minced
- 1 tablespoon lemon juice
- Salt and pepper to taste

Instructions:

Finely chop the basil leaves.

In a medium bowl, combine the mayonnaise, sour cream, minced garlic, and lemon juice.

Add the chopped basil to the bowl and stir until well combined.

Season with salt and pepper to taste.

This dip is perfect for serving with fresh vegetables, crackers, or as a topping for baked potatoes.

Dill Dip

Dill is a popular herb that has a slightly sweet, tangy flavor. It pairs well with cucumber, fish, and other seafood. To make a dill dip, you will need:

Ingredients:

- 1 cup sour cream
- 1/2 cup mayonnaise
- 1 tablespoon fresh dill, chopped

- 1 garlic clove, minced
- 1 tablespoon lemon juice
- Salt and pepper to taste

Instructions:

In a medium bowl, combine the sour cream, mayonnaise, chopped dill, minced garlic, and lemon juice.

Stir until well combined.

Season with salt and pepper to taste.

This dip is perfect for serving with raw vegetables, pita chips, or as a sauce for fish.

Mint Dip

Mint is a refreshing herb that has a sweet, cool flavor. It pairs well with lamb, cucumbers, and other Mediterranean ingredients. To make a mint dip, you will need:

Ingredients:

- 1 cup plain Greek yogurt
- 1/2 cup mayonnaise
- 2 tablespoons fresh mint, chopped
- 1 garlic clove, minced
- 1 tablespoon lemon juice
- Salt and pepper to taste

Instructions:

In a medium bowl, combine the Greek yogurt, mayonnaise, chopped mint, minced garlic, and lemon juice.

Stir until well combined.

Season with salt and pepper to taste.

This dip is perfect for serving with raw vegetables, pita chips, or as a sauce for lamb.

Rosemary Spread

Rosemary is a fragrant herb that has a strong, earthy flavor. It pairs well with roasted meats, potatoes, and other hearty dishes. To make a rosemary spread, you will need:

Ingredients:

- 8 ounces cream cheese, softened
- 1 tablespoon fresh rosemary, chopped

- 1 garlic clove, minced
- Salt and pepper to taste

Instructions:

In a medium bowl, combine the softened cream cheese, chopped rosemary, minced garlic, and a pinch of salt and pepper.

Stir until well combined.

Taste and adjust seasoning as needed.

This spread is perfect for serving with raw vegetables, crackers, or as a spread for sandwiches.

Thyme Spread

Thyme is a versatile herb that has a slightly minty, lemony flavor. It pairs well with roasted chicken and vegetables. To make a thyme spread, you will need:

Ingredients:

- 8 ounces cream cheese, softened
- 1 tablespoon fresh thyme leaves, chopped
- 1 tablespoon lemon juice
- 1 garlic clove, minced

Salt and pepper to taste

Instructions:

In a medium bowl, combine the softened cream cheese, chopped thyme leaves, lemon juice, minced garlic, and a pinch of salt and pepper.

Stir until well combined.

Taste and adjust seasoning as needed.

This spread is perfect for serving with raw vegetables, toasted bread, or as a flavorful addition to sandwiches.

Cilantro Lime Dip

Cilantro is a vibrant herb with a bright, citrusy flavor. It pairs well with Mexican and Asian dishes. To make a cilantro lime dip, you will need:

Ingredients:

- 1 cup sour cream
- 1/2 cup mayonnaise
- 1/4 cup fresh cilantro, chopped
- 2 tablespoons lime juice
- 1 garlic clove, minced
- Salt and pepper to taste

Instructions:

In a medium bowl, combine the sour cream, mayonnaise, chopped cilantro, lime juice, minced garlic, and a pinch of salt and pepper.

Stir until well combined.

Season with salt and pepper to taste.

This dip is perfect for serving with raw vegetables, tortilla chips, or as a topping for tacos and grilled meats.

Tips for Making Herb-infused Dips and Spreads

Experiment with different herb combinations: Feel free to mix and match herbs to create your own unique flavor combinations. Don't be afraid to try new herbs or adjust the quantities to suit your taste.

Use fresh herbs whenever possible: Fresh herbs have a more vibrant flavor compared to dried herbs. If fresh herbs are not available, you can use dried herbs, but remember to adjust the quantities as dried herbs are more concentrated.

Allow the flavors to meld: After preparing your herb-infused dips and spreads, let them sit in the refrigerator for at least 30 minutes to allow the flavors to meld together. This resting time will enhance the taste and aroma of the herbs.

Adjust the consistency: If you prefer a thicker dip or spread, reduce the amount of liquid ingredients such as sour cream, mayonnaise, or yogurt. If you want a thinner consistency, add a little more of the liquid ingredients or a splash of milk or cream.

Store properly: Store your herb-infused dips and spreads in airtight containers in the refrigerator. They can typically be kept for up to one week, but always check for any signs of spoilage before using.

In conclusion, herb-infused dips and spreads add a burst of fresh flavor to vegetables and can turn a simple platter of raw vegetables into a delightful and healthy appetizer. By incorporating herbs like basil, dill, mint, rosemary, thyme, and cilantro, you can create a wide range of dips and spreads that cater to various flavor preferences. Get creative, experiment with different herb combinations, and enjoy the delicious and nutritious experience of herb-infused dips and spreads with your favorite vegetables.

36. Herb-infused Dips and Spreads for Chips and Crackers

Herbs have been used in cooking for centuries, and for good reason. Not only do they add flavor and aroma to dishes, but they also offer a range of health benefits. One of the best ways to enjoy the flavors and benefits of herbs is through dips and spreads for chips and crackers. In this chapter, we'll explore some of the best herb-infused dips and spreads that are both delicious and good for you.

Before we dive into the recipes, it's worth taking a moment to talk about the benefits of herbs. For starters, many herbs are rich in antioxidants, which can help protect your body against free radicals that can cause cell damage and increase your risk of chronic diseases. Additionally, some herbs have anti-inflammatory properties, which can help reduce inflammation throughout your body and alleviate symptoms associated with conditions like arthritis, asthma, and inflammatory bowel disease.

With that in mind, let's take a look at some of the best herb-infused dips and spreads that you can make at home.

Basil and Garlic Hummus

Hummus is a classic dip that's perfect for chips, crackers, and veggies. This version features basil and garlic, two herbs that are packed with flavor and health benefits. To make it, you'll need:

- 1 can of chickpeas, drained and rinsed
- 2 cloves of garlic
- 1/4 cup of fresh basil leaves
- 1/4 cup of tahini
- 2 tablespoons of lemon juice
- 1/4 teaspoon of salt
- 1/4 teaspoon of black pepper
- 1/4 cup of olive oil

To start, place the chickpeas, garlic, basil, tahini, lemon juice, salt, and pepper in a food processor and blend until smooth. While the food processor is running, slowly drizzle in the olive oil until the mixture is creamy and well-combined. Taste and adjust the seasoning as needed, and serve with your favorite dippers.

Cilantro Lime Dip

Cilantro is a popular herb in many Latin American and Asian dishes, and it pairs perfectly with lime in this tangy dip. To make it, you'll need:

- 1/2 cup of sour cream
- 1/2 cup of Greek yogurt
- 1/4 cup of chopped cilantro
- 1 tablespoon of lime juice
- 1/4 teaspoon of salt
- 1/4 teaspoon of black pepper

To start, whisk together the sour cream, Greek yogurt, cilantro, lime juice, salt, and black pepper in a bowl until well-combined. Taste and adjust the seasoning as needed, and serve with chips, crackers, or veggies.

Rosemary and Thyme White Bean Dip

White beans are a great source of protein and fiber, and they make a delicious base for this herb-infused dip. Rosemary and thyme add a savory flavor that's perfect for pairing with crackers or toasted bread. To make it, you'll need:

- 1 can of white beans, drained and rinsed
- 1 tablespoon of fresh rosemary leaves
- 1 tablespoon of fresh thyme leaves
- 1 clove of garlic
- 2 tablespoons of lemon juice
- 1/4 cup of olive oil
- Salt and black pepper to taste

To start, place the white beans, rosemary, thyme, garlic, lemon juice, salt, and black pepper in a food processor and blend until smooth. While the food processor is running, slowly drizzle in the olive oil until the mixture is creamy and well-combined. Taste and adjust the seasoning as needed, and serve with crackers or toasted bread.

Dill and Chive Greek Yogurt Dip

Dill and chives are two classic herbs that add a fresh, bright flavor to this creamy Greek yogurt dip. This dip is perfect for serving with veggies or pita chips. To make it, you'll need:

- 1 cup of plain Greek yogurt
- 2 tablespoons of chopped fresh dill
- 2 tablespoons of chopped fresh chives

• 1 clove of garlic, minced
• 1 tablespoon of lemon juice
• Salt and black pepper to taste

To start, whisk together the Greek yogurt, dill, chives, garlic, lemon juice, salt, and black pepper in a bowl until well-combined. Taste and adjust the seasoning as needed, and serve with your favorite dippers.

Sage and Parmesan Cheese Spread

Sage is a flavorful herb that pairs perfectly with Parmesan cheese in this rich and savory spread. This spread is perfect for serving on crackers or toasted bread. To make it, you'll need:

• 1/2 cup of softened butter
• 1/2 cup of grated Parmesan cheese
• 2 tablespoons of chopped fresh sage
• 1 clove of garlic, minced
• Salt and black pepper to taste

To start, mix together the softened butter, Parmesan cheese, sage, garlic, salt, and black pepper in a bowl until well-combined. Taste and adjust the seasoning as needed, and serve on crackers or toasted bread.

These herb-infused dips and spreads are not only delicious, but they also offer a range of health benefits. By incorporating herbs into your cooking, you can add flavor and nutrition to your meals in a simple and easy way. So why not try one of these recipes the next time you're looking for a tasty and healthy snack? Your taste buds (and your body) will thank you!

Mint and Cucumber Yogurt Dip

Mint and cucumber are a classic combination that's refreshing and perfect for summer. This yogurt-based dip is great for dipping with veggies or pita chips, and it's also delicious on grilled meats or falafel. To make it, you'll need:

• 1 cup of plain Greek yogurt
• 1/2 cup of diced cucumber
• 2 tablespoons of chopped fresh mint leaves
• 1 clove of garlic, minced
• 1 tablespoon of lemon juice
• Salt and black pepper to taste

To start, whisk together the Greek yogurt, cucumber, mint, garlic, lemon juice, salt, and black pepper in a bowl until well-combined. Taste and adjust the seasoning as needed, and serve with your favorite dippers.

Parsley and Lemon Tahini Dip

Tahini is a staple in many Middle Eastern dishes, and it's a great source of protein and healthy fats. In this dip, parsley and lemon add a bright and fresh flavor that's perfect for dipping with veggies or pita chips. To make it, you'll need:

- 1/2 cup of tahini
- 1/4 cup of chopped fresh parsley
- 1 clove of garlic, minced
- 2 tablespoons of lemon juice
- 1/4 teaspoon of salt
- 1/4 teaspoon of black pepper
- Water, as needed

To start, whisk together the tahini, parsley, garlic, lemon juice, salt, and black pepper in a bowl until well-combined. Add water, 1 tablespoon at a time, until the dip reaches your desired consistency. Taste and adjust the seasoning as needed, and serve with your favorite dippers.

Tarragon Mustard Dip

Tarragon is an herb with a licorice-like flavor that pairs perfectly with mustard in this tangy dip. This dip is great for serving with pretzels, crackers, or veggies, and it's also delicious on sandwiches or grilled meats. To make it, you'll need:

- 1/2 cup of Dijon mustard
- 2 tablespoons of chopped fresh tarragon leaves
- 2 tablespoons of honey
- 1 tablespoon of apple cider vinegar
- Salt and black pepper to taste

To start, whisk together the Dijon mustard, tarragon, honey, apple cider vinegar, salt, and black pepper in a bowl until well-combined. Taste and adjust the seasoning as needed, and serve with your favorite dippers.

In conclusion, herbs are a versatile and healthy addition to any kitchen. By incorporating them into dips and spreads, you can add flavor and nutrition to your snacks and meals. These herb-infused dips and spreads are easy to make and perfect for serving with chips, crackers, or veggies. So why not try one of these recipes today and see how herbs can take your snacking game to the next level?

37. Herb-infused Dips and Spreads for Meats and Poultry

Herbs can add a depth of flavor and nutrition to meats and poultry that can make any meal memorable. In this chapter, we'll explore some delicious and easy-to-make herb-infused dips and spreads that pair perfectly with your favorite meats and poultry.

Rosemary and Garlic Butter

Rosemary is an herb that's often used in Mediterranean cooking, and it's especially delicious with roasted meats. This simple butter spread is perfect for rubbing on your favorite cuts of beef or lamb before roasting. To make it, you'll need:

- 1/2 cup of softened butter
- 2 tablespoons of chopped fresh rosemary leaves
- 2 cloves of garlic, minced
- Salt and black pepper to taste

To start, mix together the softened butter, rosemary, garlic, salt, and black pepper in a bowl until well-combined. Rub the mixture over your favorite cuts of meat before roasting, or serve alongside the meat as a spread.

Thyme and Lemon Aioli

Aioli is a traditional French sauce that's often served with seafood, but it's also delicious with chicken or pork. Thyme and lemon add a bright and fresh flavor to this classic sauce. To make it, you'll need:

- 1/2 cup of mayonnaise
- 1 clove of garlic, minced
- 2 teaspoons of chopped fresh thyme leaves
- 1 tablespoon of lemon juice
- Salt and black pepper to taste

To start, whisk together the mayonnaise, garlic, thyme, lemon juice, salt, and black pepper in a bowl until well-combined. Taste and adjust the seasoning as needed, and serve with your favorite meats or poultry.

Cilantro and Lime Chimichurri

Chimichurri is a sauce that's popular in Argentina and often served with grilled meats. This version uses cilantro and lime for a bright and fresh flavor. To make it, you'll need:

- 1 cup of fresh cilantro leaves
- 2 cloves of garlic, minced
- 1/4 cup of olive oil
- 2 tablespoons of lime juice
- 1 tablespoon of red wine vinegar
- 1/2 teaspoon of salt
- 1/4 teaspoon of black pepper

To start, pulse the cilantro, garlic, olive oil, lime juice, red wine vinegar, salt, and black pepper in a food processor until well-combined but still slightly chunky. Taste and adjust the seasoning as needed, and serve with your favorite grilled meats or poultry.

Sage and Walnut Pesto

Pesto is a classic Italian sauce that's traditionally made with basil, but this version uses sage and walnuts for a unique twist. This pesto is great for serving with pork or turkey. To make it, you'll need:

- 1 cup of fresh sage leaves
- 1/2 cup of chopped walnuts
- 1/2 cup of grated Parmesan cheese
- 2 cloves of garlic, minced
- 1/4 cup of olive oil
- Salt and black pepper to taste

To start, pulse the sage, walnuts, Parmesan cheese, garlic, olive oil, salt, and black pepper in a food processor until well-combined but still slightly chunky. Taste and adjust the seasoning as needed, and serve with your favorite meats or poultry.

Basil and Sun-Dried Tomato Butter

Basil and sun-dried tomatoes are a classic Italian combination that's perfect for adding flavor to grilled meats or chicken. This simple butter spread is easy to make and packed with flavor. To make it, you'll need:

- 1/2 cup of softened butter
- 2 tablespoons of chopped fresh basil leaves
- 2 tablespoons of chopped sun-dried tomatoes

- Salt and black pepper to taste

To start, mix together the softened butter, basil, sun-dried tomatoes, salt, and black pepper in a bowl until well-combined. Rub the mixture over your favorite cuts of meat before grilling, or serve alongside the meat as a spread.

Tarragon and Mustard Sauce

Tarragon is an herb that's often used in French cooking and pairs perfectly with poultry. This sauce combines tarragon with Dijon mustard and white wine for a tangy and flavorful sauce. To make it, you'll need:

- 1/2 cup of mayonnaise
- 2 tablespoons of chopped fresh tarragon leaves
- 2 tablespoons of Dijon mustard
- 2 tablespoons of white wine vinegar
- Salt and black pepper to taste

To start, whisk together the mayonnaise, tarragon, Dijon mustard, white wine vinegar, salt, and black pepper in a bowl until well-combined. Taste and adjust the seasoning as needed, and serve with your favorite poultry.

Parsley and Lemon Gremolata

Gremolata is a classic Italian sauce that's traditionally served with osso buco, but it's also delicious with roasted or grilled meats. This version uses parsley and lemon for a bright and fresh flavor. To make it, you'll need:

- 1/2 cup of chopped fresh parsley leaves
- 2 cloves of garlic, minced
- 1 tablespoon of lemon zest
- Salt and black pepper to taste

To start, mix together the chopped parsley, minced garlic, lemon zest, salt, and black pepper in a bowl until well-combined. Sprinkle the mixture over your favorite roasted or grilled meats before serving.

In conclusion, herbs are a wonderful addition to any meat or poultry dish, and these herb-infused dips and spreads are a great way to add even more flavor and nutrition. Whether you're grilling, roasting, or sautéing, there's an herb-infused dip or spread that's perfect for your meal. So go ahead and experiment with different combinations of herbs and flavors to create your own delicious and healthy dishes!

38. Herb-infused Dips and Spreads for Seafood

Seafood is a delicious and healthy protein source, but sometimes it can be a bit bland on its own. That's where herb-infused dips and spreads come in! By combining fresh herbs with creamy dips or tangy sauces, you can add a burst of flavor to any seafood dish. In this chapter, we'll explore some of the best herb-infused dips and spreads for seafood.

Cilantro Lime Crema

Cilantro and lime are a classic flavor combination that works beautifully with seafood. This crema is creamy, tangy, and packed with fresh herb flavor. To make it, you'll need:

- 1/2 cup of sour cream
- 1/2 cup of mayonnaise
- 1/4 cup of chopped fresh cilantro leaves
- 1 tablespoon of lime zest
- 1 tablespoon of lime juice

Salt and black pepper to taste

To start, whisk together the sour cream, mayonnaise, chopped cilantro, lime zest, lime juice, salt, and black pepper in a bowl until well-combined. Taste and adjust the seasoning as needed, and serve with your favorite seafood.

Lemon Dill Sauce

Dill is a classic herb that pairs perfectly with seafood, and this sauce is no exception. The lemon adds a bright, citrusy note that balances the richness of the fish. To make it, you'll need:

- 1/2 cup of mayonnaise
- 1/4 cup of sour cream
- 2 tablespoons of chopped fresh dill leaves
- 1 tablespoon of lemon zest
- 1 tablespoon of lemon juice
- Salt and black pepper to taste

To start, whisk together the mayonnaise, sour cream, chopped dill, lemon zest, lemon juice, salt, and black pepper in a bowl until well-combined. Taste and adjust the seasoning as needed, and serve with your favorite seafood.

Basil Pesto

Pesto is a classic Italian sauce that's traditionally made with basil, garlic, pine nuts, and Parmesan cheese. It's delicious on pasta, but it also works beautifully with seafood. To make it, you'll need:

- 2 cups of fresh basil leaves
- 1/2 cup of pine nuts
- 2 cloves of garlic, minced
- 1/2 cup of grated Parmesan cheese
- 1/2 cup of olive oil
- Salt and black pepper to taste

To start, combine the basil leaves, pine nuts, minced garlic, and Parmesan cheese in a food processor. Pulse until the ingredients are well-combined, then gradually add the olive oil while continuing to pulse. Taste and adjust the seasoning as needed, and serve with your favorite seafood.

Garlic and Herb Butter

Butter is a simple and delicious way to add flavor to any seafood dish, and this garlic and herb butter takes things to the next level. To make it, you'll need:

- 1/2 cup of softened butter
- 2 cloves of garlic, minced
- 2 tablespoons of chopped fresh parsley leaves
- 2 tablespoons of chopped fresh chives
- Salt and black pepper to taste

To start, mix together the softened butter, minced garlic, chopped parsley, chopped chives, salt, and black pepper in a bowl until well-combined. Spread the mixture over your favorite seafood before grilling, or serve alongside the seafood as a spread.

Roasted Red Pepper and Feta Dip

Roasted red peppers add a smoky and sweet flavor to this creamy dip, while feta cheese adds a tangy note that works beautifully with seafood. To make it, you'll need:

- 1 cup of roasted red peppers
- 1/2 cup of crumbled feta cheese
- 1/4 cup of mayonnaise
- 1/4 cup of sour cream
- 1 tablespoon of chopped fresh parsley leaves
- 1 clove of garlic, minced

- Salt and black pepper to taste

To start, puree the roasted red peppers in a food processor until smooth. Add the crumbled feta cheese, mayonnaise, sour cream, chopped parsley, minced garlic, salt, and black pepper, and pulse until the ingredients are well-combined. Taste and adjust the seasoning as needed, and serve with your favorite seafood.

Horseradish Cream Sauce

Horseradish has a strong, spicy flavor that adds a unique kick to seafood dishes. This cream sauce balances out the heat with the richness of sour cream and the fresh flavor of dill. To make it, you'll need:

- 1/2 cup of sour cream
- 2 tablespoons of prepared horseradish
- 1 tablespoon of chopped fresh dill leaves
- 1 teaspoon of Dijon mustard
- Salt and black pepper to taste

To start, whisk together the sour cream, prepared horseradish, chopped dill, Dijon mustard, salt, and black pepper in a bowl until well-combined. Taste and adjust the seasoning as needed, and serve with your favorite seafood.

Chimichurri Sauce

Chimichurri is a bright and tangy sauce that's traditionally served with grilled meats in Argentina. However, it also works beautifully with seafood, adding a burst of fresh herb flavor to any dish. To make it, you'll need:

- 1 cup of fresh parsley leaves
- 1/4 cup of fresh oregano leaves
- 2 cloves of garlic, minced
- 1/4 cup of red wine vinegar
- 1/2 cup of olive oil
- Salt and black pepper to taste

To start, combine the parsley leaves, oregano leaves, minced garlic, red wine vinegar, salt, and black pepper in a food processor. Pulse until the ingredients are well-combined, then gradually add the olive oil while continuing to pulse. Taste and adjust the seasoning as needed, and serve with your favorite seafood.

In conclusion, herb-infused dips and spreads are a delicious and easy way to add flavor to any seafood dish. From classic flavors like cilantro lime and lemon dill to more unique options like roasted red pepper and horseradish cream, there's a dip or spread out there for every seafood lover. So next time you're looking to add a little something extra to your seafood meal, consider whipping up one of these tasty herb-infused dips or spreads.

39. Herb-infused Dips and Spreads for Breads and Rolls

Breads and rolls are staples in many cuisines around the world, but they can sometimes feel a bit plain on their own. That's where herb-infused dips and spreads come in. With just a few simple ingredients, you can transform a plain roll or slice of bread into a flavor-packed snack or appetizer. In this chapter, we'll explore some of the best herb-infused dips and spreads for breads and rolls.

Garlic and Herb Butter

Garlic and herb butter is a classic spread that's perfect for rolls and breads. The garlic gives it a bold, savory flavor, while the herbs add a fresh and bright note. To make it, you'll need:

- 1/2 cup of unsalted butter, softened
- 2 cloves of garlic, minced
- 1 tablespoon of chopped fresh parsley leaves
- 1 tablespoon of chopped fresh thyme leaves
- Salt and black pepper to taste

To start, combine the softened butter, minced garlic, chopped parsley, chopped thyme, salt, and black pepper in a bowl. Use a fork or whisk to mix everything together until well-combined. Taste and adjust the seasoning as needed, and spread the mixture onto your favorite rolls or slices of bread.

Sundried Tomato and Basil Spread

This spread combines the sweetness of sundried tomatoes with the fresh flavor of basil. It's perfect for adding a burst of flavor to any bread or roll. To make it, you'll need:

- 1/2 cup of sundried tomatoes, packed in oil
- 1/2 cup of cream cheese, softened
- 1/4 cup of chopped fresh basil leaves
- 1 clove of garlic, minced
- Salt and black pepper to taste

To start, drain the oil from the sundried tomatoes and chop them into small pieces. In a bowl, combine the chopped sundried tomatoes, softened cream cheese, chopped basil, minced garlic, salt, and black pepper. Mix everything together until well-combined. Taste and adjust the seasoning as needed, and spread the mixture onto your favorite breads and rolls.

Cilantro Lime Spread

This spread is inspired by the flavors of Mexico, with the bright citrus flavor of lime and the fresh taste of cilantro. It's perfect for adding a bit of zing to any bread or roll. To make it, you'll need:

- 1/2 cup of cream cheese, softened
- 2 tablespoons of chopped fresh cilantro leaves
- 1 tablespoon of lime juice
- 1/4 teaspoon of cumin powder
- Salt and black pepper to taste

To start, combine the softened cream cheese, chopped cilantro, lime juice, cumin powder, salt, and black pepper in a bowl. Mix everything together until well-combined. Taste and adjust the seasoning as needed, and spread the mixture onto your favorite breads and rolls.

Roasted Garlic and Rosemary Dip

Roasted garlic has a sweet and nutty flavor that pairs perfectly with the earthy taste of rosemary. This dip is perfect for serving with crusty breads or rolls. To make it, you'll need:

- 1/2 cup of sour cream
- 1/2 cup of mayonnaise
- 1 head of garlic, roasted
- 1 tablespoon of chopped fresh rosemary leaves
- Salt and black pepper to taste

To start, roast the head of garlic in the oven until it's soft and fragrant. Once it's cool enough to handle, squeeze the cloves out of their skins and chop them into small pieces. In a bowl, combine the sour cream, mayonnaise, chopped roasted garlic, chopped rosemary, salt, and black pepper. Mix everything together until well-combined. Taste and adjust the seasoning as needed, and serve with your favorite breads and rolls.

Lemon and Dill Spread

This spread is light and refreshing, with the zesty flavor of lemon and the fresh taste of dill. It's perfect for serving with crusty breads or rolls. To make it, you'll need:

- 1/2 cup of cream cheese, softened

- 2 tablespoons of chopped fresh dill leaves
- 1 tablespoon of lemon zest
- 1 tablespoon of lemon juice
- Salt and black pepper to taste

To start, combine the softened cream cheese, chopped dill, lemon zest, lemon juice, salt, and black pepper in a bowl. Mix everything together until well-combined. Taste and adjust the seasoning as needed, and spread the mixture onto your favorite breads and rolls.

Olive Tapenade

Olive tapenade is a classic spread that's perfect for serving with crusty breads or rolls. It's made with a combination of olives, capers, and herbs, and has a bold and savory flavor. To make it, you'll need:

- 1 cup of pitted black olives
- 2 tablespoons of capers
- 2 cloves of garlic, minced
- 1/4 cup of chopped fresh parsley leaves
- 1/4 cup of chopped fresh basil leaves
- 1/4 cup of extra-virgin olive oil
- Salt and black pepper to taste

To start, combine the black olives, capers, minced garlic, chopped parsley, chopped basil, and extra-virgin olive oil in a food processor. Pulse the mixture until it forms a chunky paste. Taste and adjust the seasoning as needed, and spread the mixture onto your favorite breads and rolls.

Pesto Dip

Pesto is a classic Italian sauce that's perfect for serving with breads or rolls. It's made with a combination of fresh herbs, nuts, and cheese, and has a bright and herbaceous flavor. To make it, you'll need:

- 1 cup of fresh basil leaves
- 1/4 cup of pine nuts
- 1/4 cup of grated Parmesan cheese
- 2 cloves of garlic, minced
- 1/4 cup of extra-virgin olive oil
- Salt and black pepper to taste

To start, combine the fresh basil leaves, pine nuts, grated Parmesan cheese, minced garlic, and extra-virgin olive oil in a food processor. Pulse the mixture until it forms a smooth paste. Taste and adjust the seasoning as needed, and serve with your favorite breads and rolls.

In conclusion, herb-infused dips and spreads are a great way to add flavor and interest to breads and rolls. From classic garlic and herb butter to zesty cilantro lime spread, there are endless possibilities for creating delicious dips and spreads. By incorporating fresh herbs into your spreads, you'll also be adding a healthy dose of vitamins and antioxidants to your diet. So next time you're looking to spruce up your bread or roll game, try one of these herb-infused dips or spreads for a delicious and healthy snack or appetizer.

40. Herb-infused Dips and Spreads for Pasta and Noodles

Pasta and noodles are a versatile and satisfying base for a variety of dishes. Adding herb-infused dips and spreads to your pasta and noodle dishes is a great way to elevate their flavor and make them more interesting. In this chapter, we'll explore some delicious herb-infused dips and spreads that are perfect for pasta and noodles.

Basil Pesto

Basil pesto is a classic Italian sauce that's perfect for tossing with pasta or noodles. It's made with fresh basil leaves, pine nuts, garlic, Parmesan cheese, and olive oil, and has a bright and herbaceous flavor. To make it, you'll need:

- 2 cups of fresh basil leaves
- 1/2 cup of pine nuts
- 1/2 cup of grated Parmesan cheese
- 3 cloves of garlic, minced
- 1/2 cup of extra-virgin olive oil
- Salt and black pepper to taste

To start, combine the basil leaves, pine nuts, Parmesan cheese, and minced garlic in a food processor. Pulse the mixture until it forms a coarse paste. With the food processor running, slowly drizzle in the olive oil until the mixture forms a smooth paste. Season with salt and black pepper to taste, and toss with your favorite cooked pasta or noodles.

Roasted Red Pepper Sauce

Roasted red pepper sauce is a delicious and versatile sauce that's perfect for pasta or noodles. It's made with roasted red peppers, garlic, cream cheese, and herbs, and has a rich and smoky flavor. To make it, you'll need:

- 2 large red bell peppers, roasted and peeled
- 2 cloves of garlic, minced
- 4 ounces of cream cheese, softened
- 2 tablespoons of chopped fresh parsley
- 2 tablespoons of chopped fresh basil
- Salt and black pepper to taste

To start, blend the roasted red peppers, minced garlic, and softened cream cheese in a blender or food processor until smooth. Stir in the chopped parsley, chopped basil, salt, and black pepper. Heat the sauce in a saucepan over medium heat until warmed through, and toss with your favorite cooked pasta or noodles.

Lemon and Herb Sauce

Lemon and herb sauce is a light and refreshing sauce that's perfect for pasta or noodles. It's made with fresh herbs, lemon juice, olive oil, and garlic, and has a bright and tangy flavor. To make it, you'll need:

- 1/2 cup of fresh parsley leaves
- 1/4 cup of fresh basil leaves
- 1/4 cup of fresh mint leaves
- 2 cloves of garlic, minced
- 1/4 cup of extra-virgin olive oil
- 2 tablespoons of lemon juice
- Salt and black pepper to taste

To start, combine the fresh parsley leaves, basil leaves, mint leaves, and minced garlic in a food processor. Pulse the mixture until it forms a coarse paste. With the food processor running, slowly drizzle in the olive oil until the mixture forms a smooth paste. Stir in the lemon juice, salt, and black pepper. Toss with your favorite cooked pasta or noodles.

Spicy Arrabbiata Sauce

Arrabbiata sauce is a spicy Italian tomato sauce that's perfect for pasta or noodles. It's made with canned tomatoes, garlic, red pepper flakes, and herbs, and has a bold and spicy flavor. To make it, you'll need:

- 2 cans of whole peeled tomatoes
- 4 cloves of garlic, minced
- 1 teaspoon of red pepper flakes
- 2 tablespoons of chopped fresh parsley
- 2 tablespoons of chopped fresh basil
- Salt and black pepper to taste

To start, heat some olive oil in a large saucepan over medium heat. Add the minced garlic and red pepper flakes, and sauté for a minute or two until fragrant. Add the canned tomatoes, and break them up with a wooden spoon. Add the chopped parsley, chopped basil, salt, and black pepper, and simmer the sauce for about 15-20 minutes, or until it thickens and the flavors meld together. Serve over your favorite cooked pasta or noodles.

Garlic and Herb Butter

Garlic and herb butter is a simple yet delicious spread that's perfect for tossing with pasta or noodles. It's made with butter, garlic, and herbs, and has a rich and savory flavor. To make it, you'll need:

- 1/2 cup of unsalted butter, softened
- 4 cloves of garlic, minced
- 2 tablespoons of chopped fresh parsley
- 2 tablespoons of chopped fresh basil
- Salt and black pepper to taste

To start, combine the softened butter, minced garlic, chopped parsley, chopped basil, salt, and black pepper in a bowl. Use a fork to mash the ingredients together until they're well combined. Toss with your favorite cooked pasta or noodles.

Cilantro Lime Sauce

Cilantro lime sauce is a tangy and flavorful sauce that's perfect for pasta or noodles. It's made with fresh cilantro, lime juice, garlic, and olive oil, and has a bright and zesty flavor. To make it, you'll need:

- 1/2 cup of fresh cilantro leaves
- 2 cloves of garlic, minced
- 1/4 cup of extra-virgin olive oil
- 2 tablespoons of lime juice
- Salt and black pepper to taste

To start, combine the fresh cilantro leaves, minced garlic, and extra-virgin olive oil in a food processor. Pulse the mixture until it forms a coarse paste. Stir in the lime juice, salt, and black pepper. Toss with your favorite cooked pasta or noodles.

Sun-Dried Tomato Pesto

Sun-dried tomato pesto is a flavorful and versatile spread that's perfect for pasta or noodles. It's made with sun-dried tomatoes, garlic, Parmesan cheese, and herbs, and has a rich and savory flavor. To make it, you'll need:

- 1 cup of sun-dried tomatoes, packed in oil
- 2 cloves of garlic, minced
- 1/2 cup of grated Parmesan cheese

- 1/4 cup of chopped fresh basil
- 1/4 cup of chopped fresh parsley
- 1/2 cup of extra-virgin olive oil
- Salt and black pepper to taste

To start, drain the sun-dried tomatoes and reserve the oil. Combine the sun-dried tomatoes, minced garlic, grated Parmesan cheese, chopped basil, chopped parsley, and some of the reserved oil in a food processor. Pulse the mixture until it forms a coarse paste. With the food processor running, slowly drizzle in the extra-virgin olive oil until the mixture forms a smooth paste. Season with salt and black pepper to taste, and toss with your favorite cooked pasta or noodles.

In conclusion, adding herb-infused dips and spreads to your pasta and noodle dishes is a great way to add flavor and variety to your meals. Whether you prefer a classic pesto or a spicy arrabbiata sauce, there's a herb-infused dip or spread that's perfect for your tastes. So go ahead and experiment with different herbs and flavors to find your favorite combination!

41. Herb-infused Dips and Spreads for Rice and Grains

Rice and grains are versatile ingredients that can be transformed with the addition of herb-infused dips and spreads. Whether you're making a simple rice bowl or a complex grain salad, there's a herb-infused dip or spread that can add flavor and complexity to your dish. In this chapter, we'll explore some of the best herb-infused dips and spreads for rice and grains.

Herbed Yogurt Sauce

Herbed yogurt sauce is a simple and healthy dip that's perfect for rice and grain bowls. It's made with plain yogurt, fresh herbs, and lemon juice, and has a tangy and refreshing flavor. To make it, you'll need:

- 1 cup of plain Greek yogurt
- 1/4 cup of chopped fresh herbs (such as parsley, dill, and mint)
- 1 tablespoon of lemon juice
- Salt and black pepper to taste

To start, combine the plain Greek yogurt, chopped fresh herbs, lemon juice, salt, and black pepper in a bowl. Mix well to combine. Serve with rice and grains.

Green Goddess Dressing

Green goddess dressing is a classic herb-infused dressing that's perfect for rice and grain salads. It's made with fresh herbs, garlic, anchovies, and mayonnaise, and has a rich and tangy flavor. To make it, you'll need:

- 1/2 cup of chopped fresh herbs (such as parsley, tarragon, and chives)
- 2 cloves of garlic, minced
- 2 anchovy fillets, minced
- 1/4 cup of mayonnaise
- 2 tablespoons of sour cream
- 2 tablespoons of lemon juice
- Salt and black pepper to taste

To start, combine the chopped fresh herbs, minced garlic, minced anchovy fillets, mayonnaise, sour cream, and lemon juice in a food processor. Pulse the mixture until it forms a smooth paste. Season with salt and black pepper to taste. Serve with rice and grain salads.

Spicy Harissa Sauce

Spicy harissa sauce is a flavorful and fiery dip that's perfect for rice and grain bowls. It's made with hot peppers, garlic, and spices, and has a bold and smoky flavor. To make it, you'll need:

- 6-8 dried hot peppers (such as Guajillo or New Mexico)
- 2 cloves of garlic
- 1 teaspoon of ground cumin
- 1 teaspoon of ground coriander
- 1/2 teaspoon of smoked paprika
- 1/4 cup of extra-virgin olive oil
- Salt and black pepper to taste

To start, soak the dried hot peppers in hot water for 30 minutes to soften them. Drain the peppers and remove the stems and seeds. Combine the softened peppers, garlic, ground cumin, ground coriander, smoked paprika, extra-virgin olive oil, salt, and black pepper in a food processor. Pulse the mixture until it forms a smooth paste. Serve with rice and grain bowls.

Lemon Herb Butter

Lemon herb butter is a rich and tangy spread that's perfect for rice and grains. It's made with butter, lemon zest, and fresh herbs, and has a bright and refreshing flavor. To make it, you'll need:

- 1/2 cup of unsalted butter, softened
- 1 tablespoon of lemon zest
- 2 tablespoons of chopped fresh herbs (such as thyme, rosemary, and oregano)
- Salt and black pepper to taste

To start, combine the softened butter, lemon zest, chopped fresh herbs, salt, and black pepper in a bowl. Use a fork to mash the ingredients together until well combined. Serve with rice and grains.

Basil Pesto

Basil pesto is a classic herb-infused spread that's perfect for pasta and noodles, but it also works well with rice and grains. It's made with fresh basil, garlic, pine nuts, and Parmesan cheese, and has a rich and savory flavor. To make it, you'll need:

- 2 cups of fresh basil leaves, packed
- 3 cloves of garlic
- 1/2 cup of pine nuts, toasted

- 1/2 cup of grated Parmesan cheese
- 1/2 cup of extra-virgin olive oil
- Salt and black pepper to taste

To start, combine the fresh basil leaves, garlic, toasted pine nuts, grated Parmesan cheese, salt, and black pepper in a food processor. Pulse the mixture until it forms a coarse paste. With the food processor running, slowly drizzle in the extra-virgin olive oil until the pesto is smooth and creamy. Serve with rice and grains.

Ginger Soy Dressing

Ginger soy dressing is a tangy and savory dip that's perfect for rice and grain bowls. It's made with ginger, soy sauce, rice vinegar, and sesame oil, and has a bright and bold flavor. To make it, you'll need:

- 2 tablespoons of grated fresh ginger
- 2 tablespoons of soy sauce
- 2 tablespoons of rice vinegar
- 1 tablespoon of honey
- 1 tablespoon of sesame oil
- 1 clove of garlic, minced
- Salt and black pepper to taste

To start, combine the grated fresh ginger, soy sauce, rice vinegar, honey, sesame oil, minced garlic, salt, and black pepper in a bowl. Whisk the ingredients together until well combined. Serve with rice and grain bowls.

Cilantro Lime Crema

Cilantro lime crema is a tangy and creamy dip that's perfect for rice and grain bowls. It's made with sour cream, fresh cilantro, lime juice, and garlic, and has a zesty and refreshing flavor. To make it, you'll need:

- 1 cup of sour cream
- 1/4 cup of chopped fresh cilantro
- 1 tablespoon of lime juice
- 1 clove of garlic, minced
- Salt and black pepper to taste

To start, combine the sour cream, chopped fresh cilantro, lime juice, minced garlic, salt, and black pepper in a bowl. Mix well to combine. Serve with rice and grain bowls.

In conclusion, herb-infused dips and spreads are an easy and delicious way to add flavor and complexity to your rice and grain dishes. Whether you prefer tangy yogurt sauces or bold and fiery harissa, there's a herb-infused dip or spread that can take your rice and grain dishes to the next level. Experiment with different herbs and spices to create your own unique dips and spreads, and enjoy the health benefits and flavor that herbs can bring to your cooking.

42. Herb-infused Smoothie and Juice Recipes

Smoothies and juices are a delicious and healthy way to incorporate herbs into your diet. Herbs are packed with nutrients and antioxidants, and adding them to your drinks can give your body a boost of flavor and nutrition. In this chapter, we'll explore some of the best herb-infused smoothie and juice recipes that you can make at home.

Green Goddess Smoothie

This smoothie is packed with nutrients and flavor, thanks to the combination of herbs and leafy greens. To make it, you'll need:

- 1/2 cup of fresh parsley leaves
- 1/2 cup of fresh mint leaves
- 1/2 cup of fresh basil leaves
- 1/2 cup of fresh spinach leaves
- 1/2 cup of fresh kale leaves
- 1 cup of coconut water
- 1/2 cup of frozen pineapple chunks
- 1/2 cup of frozen mango chunks
- 1 banana, sliced

To start, combine the fresh parsley leaves, mint leaves, basil leaves, spinach leaves, kale leaves, and coconut water in a blender. Blend until the mixture is smooth and well combined. Add the frozen pineapple chunks, frozen mango chunks, and sliced banana to the blender, and blend again until the smoothie is thick and creamy. Serve immediately.

Lemon and Thyme Juice

This juice is refreshing and tangy, thanks to the combination of lemon and thyme. To make it, you'll need:

- 1/2 cup of fresh thyme leaves
- 1/2 cup of freshly squeezed lemon juice
- 2 cups of filtered water
- 1 tablespoon of honey (optional)

To start, combine the fresh thyme leaves, freshly squeezed lemon juice, filtered water, and honey (if using) in a blender. Blend until the mixture is well combined and the thyme leaves are finely chopped. Strain the mixture through a fine-mesh strainer into a glass, and discard the thyme leaves. Serve the juice chilled or over ice.

Strawberry and Basil Smoothie

This smoothie is sweet and herbaceous, thanks to the combination of strawberries and basil. To make it, you'll need:

- 2 cups of frozen strawberries
- 1/2 cup of fresh basil leaves
- 1/2 cup of plain Greek yogurt
- 1/2 cup of almond milk
- 1 tablespoon of honey (optional)

To start, combine the frozen strawberries, fresh basil leaves, plain Greek yogurt, almond milk, and honey (if using) in a blender. Blend until the mixture is smooth and well combined. Serve immediately.

Cucumber and Mint Juice

This juice is refreshing and hydrating, thanks to the combination of cucumber and mint. To make it, you'll need:

- 1 large cucumber, peeled and chopped
- 1/2 cup of fresh mint leaves
- 2 cups of filtered water
- 1 tablespoon of honey (optional)

To start, combine the chopped cucumber, fresh mint leaves, filtered water, and honey (if using) in a blender. Blend until the mixture is well combined and the cucumber is finely chopped. Strain the mixture through a fine-mesh strainer into a glass, and discard the cucumber and mint leaves. Serve the juice chilled or over ice.

Pineapple and Sage Smoothie

This smoothie is tropical and herbaceous, thanks to the combination of pineapple and sage. To make it, you'll need:

- 2 cups of frozen pineapple chunks
- 1/2 cup of fresh sage leaves
- 1 cup of coconut water
- 1/2 cup of plain Greek yogurt
- 1 tablespoon of honey (optional)

To start, combine the frozen pineapple chunks, fresh sage leaves, coconut water, plain Greek yogurt, and honey (if using) in a blender. Blend until the mixture is smooth and well combined. Serve immediately.

Watermelon and Basil Juice

This juice is light and refreshing, thanks to the combination of watermelon and basil. To make it, you'll need:

- 4 cups of chopped seedless watermelon
- 1/2 cup of fresh basil leaves
- 2 tablespoons of freshly squeezed lime juice
- 1 tablespoon of honey (optional)

To start, combine the chopped watermelon, fresh basil leaves, lime juice, and honey (if using) in a blender. Blend until the mixture is well combined and the watermelon is fully blended. Strain the mixture through a fine-mesh strainer into a glass, and discard any solids. Serve the juice chilled or over ice.

Blueberry and Lavender Smoothie

This smoothie is vibrant and floral, thanks to the combination of blueberries and lavender. To make it, you'll need:

- 2 cups of frozen blueberries
- 1/2 cup of fresh lavender flowers (or 1 teaspoon of dried lavender)
- 1 cup of almond milk
- 1 tablespoon of honey (optional)

To start, combine the frozen blueberries, fresh lavender flowers (or dried lavender), almond milk, and honey (if using) in a blender. Blend until the mixture is smooth and well combined. Serve immediately.

In conclusion, herb-infused smoothies and juices are a fantastic way to enjoy the health benefits and flavors of herbs. From the green goodness of parsley and mint to the zesty combination of lemon and thyme, these recipes offer a wide range of options for incorporating herbs into your drinks. Whether you're looking for a refreshing juice or a creamy smoothie, the herb-infused recipes in this chapter will satisfy your taste buds and provide a nutritional boost. So, grab your blender, gather some fresh herbs, and start creating these delicious and nourishing herb-infused smoothies and juices in the comfort of your own kitchen.

43. Herb-infused Tea and Coffee Recipes

When it comes to beverages, tea and coffee are two of the most popular options. Not only are they enjoyed for their taste and aroma, but they also offer a range of health benefits. By infusing these drinks with herbs, you can elevate their flavors and add even more nutritional value. In this chapter, we'll explore a variety of herb-infused tea and coffee recipes that are easy to make and delicious to drink.

Mint Tea

Mint tea is a refreshing and calming drink that's perfect for any time of day. To make it, you'll need:

- 2 cups of water
- 1/4 cup of fresh mint leaves
- 1 tablespoon of honey (optional)

To start, bring the water to a boil in a saucepan. Add the fresh mint leaves and let them steep for about 5 minutes. Remove the pan from heat and let it sit for another 5 minutes to allow the flavors to infuse. Strain the mixture through a fine-mesh strainer into a mug, and add honey to taste (if using). Serve hot or chilled.

Ginger Tea

Ginger tea is a spicy and warming drink that's great for digestion and inflammation. To make it, you'll need:

- 2 cups of water
- 1/4 cup of fresh ginger root, peeled and sliced
- 1 tablespoon of honey (optional)

To start, bring the water to a boil in a saucepan. Add the fresh ginger slices and let them steep for about 5 minutes. Remove the pan from heat and let it sit for another 5 minutes to allow the flavors to infuse. Strain the mixture through a fine-mesh strainer into a mug, and add honey to taste (if using). Serve hot.

Rosemary Coffee

Rosemary coffee is a unique and savory drink that pairs well with breakfast dishes. To make it, you'll need:

- 2 cups of brewed coffee
- 1 tablespoon of fresh rosemary leaves

- 1 tablespoon of honey (optional)

To start, brew the coffee according to your preference. Add the fresh rosemary leaves to the brewed coffee and let it steep for about 5 minutes. Strain the mixture through a fine-mesh strainer into a mug, and add honey to taste (if using). Serve hot.

Lavender Latte

Lavender latte is a floral and soothing drink that's perfect for a relaxing afternoon. To make it, you'll need:

- 1 shot of espresso (or 1/2 cup of brewed coffee)
- 1 cup of milk (dairy or non-dairy)
- 1 tablespoon of culinary lavender buds
- 1 tablespoon of honey (optional)

To start, heat the milk in a small saucepan until it's hot but not boiling. Add the culinary lavender buds and let them steep for about 5 minutes. Strain the mixture through a fine-mesh strainer into a mug. Brew a shot of espresso (or use 1/2 cup of brewed coffee) and add it to the mug. Add honey to taste (if using) and stir to combine.

Lemon and Thyme Tea

Lemon and thyme tea is a zesty and fragrant drink that's great for boosting the immune system. To make it, you'll need:

- 2 cups of water
- 1/4 cup of fresh thyme sprigs
- Juice of 1 lemon
- 1 tablespoon of honey (optional)

To start, bring the water to a boil in a saucepan. Add the fresh thyme sprigs and let them steep for about 5 minutes. Remove the pan from heat and let it sit for another 5 minutes to allow the flavors to infuse. Stir in the lemon juice and honey to taste (if using). Strain the mixture through a fine-mesh strainer into a mug. Serve hot or chilled.

Chamomile and Orange Infusion

Chamomile and orange infusion is a soothing and citrusy drink that's perfect for winding down in the evening. To make it, you'll need:

- 2 cups of water
- 2 chamomile tea bags
- Peel of 1 orange

• 1 tablespoon of honey (optional)

To start, bring the water to a boil in a saucepan. Add the chamomile tea bags and orange peel, and let them steep for about 5 minutes. Remove the pan from heat and let it sit for another 5 minutes to allow the flavors to infuse. Remove the tea bags and orange peel. Stir in honey to taste (if using). Serve hot or chilled.

Hibiscus Iced Tea

Hibiscus iced tea is a vibrant and refreshing drink that's packed with antioxidants. To make it, you'll need:

• 4 cups of water
• 1/4 cup of dried hibiscus flowers
• Juice of 1 lemon
• 1 tablespoon of honey (optional)
• Ice cubes

To start, bring the water to a boil in a saucepan. Add the dried hibiscus flowers and let them steep for about 10 minutes. Remove the pan from heat and let it cool completely. Strain the mixture through a fine-mesh strainer into a pitcher. Stir in the lemon juice and honey to taste (if using). Refrigerate until chilled. Serve over ice.

In conclusion, herb-infused tea and coffee recipes offer a delightful way to enjoy the benefits of herbs while savoring your favorite hot or cold beverages. From the refreshing and calming qualities of mint tea to the aromatic and invigorating flavors of rosemary coffee, these recipes showcase the versatility of herbs in creating unique and delicious drinks. Whether you're looking to boost your immune system, relax in the evening, or simply enjoy a flavorful twist on your everyday beverages, these herb-infused tea and coffee recipes are sure to please. So, gather your herbs, brew a pot of tea, or prepare a cup of coffee, and experience the delightful infusion of herbs in your favorite drinks. Cheers to flavor and health!

44. Herb-infused Iced Beverages

As the temperatures rise during summer, nothing beats a refreshing and flavorful iced beverage. Adding herbs to your drinks not only enhances the taste but also provides numerous health benefits. In this chapter, we will explore a variety of herb-infused iced beverage recipes that will keep you cool, hydrated, and healthy during the hot summer months.

Lavender Lemonade

Lavender lemonade is a popular drink that combines the tangy taste of lemon with the calming scent of lavender. To make it, you'll need:

- 1 cup of fresh lemon juice
- 1/2 cup of honey
- 8 cups of water
- 1/4 cup of dried culinary lavender flowers
- Ice cubes
- Lemon slices and fresh lavender sprigs for garnish (optional)

To start, bring the water to a boil in a saucepan. Add the dried lavender flowers and let them steep for about 10 minutes. Remove the pan from heat and let it cool completely. Strain the mixture through a fine-mesh strainer into a pitcher. Stir in the lemon juice and honey until well combined. Refrigerate until chilled. Serve over ice with lemon slices and fresh lavender sprigs for garnish (if using).

Minty Watermelon Refresher

Minty watermelon refresher is a sweet and refreshing drink that's perfect for a hot summer day. To make it, you'll need:

- 6 cups of cubed watermelon
- 1/4 cup of fresh mint leaves
- 1/4 cup of honey
- 1/4 cup of fresh lime juice
- 2 cups of cold water
- Ice cubes
- Mint sprigs for garnish (optional)

To start, add the cubed watermelon, mint leaves, honey, and lime juice to a blender. Blend until smooth. Strain the mixture through a fine-mesh strainer into a pitcher. Stir in the cold water until well combined. Refrigerate until chilled. Serve over ice with mint sprigs for garnish (if using).

Ginger Peach Iced Tea

Ginger peach iced tea is a refreshing and energizing drink that's perfect for a hot summer afternoon. To make it, you'll need:

- 6 cups of water
- 4 black tea bags
- 2 peaches, pitted and sliced
- 1/4 cup of fresh ginger, peeled and sliced
- 1/4 cup of honey
- Ice cubes
- Peach slices and fresh ginger slices for garnish (optional)

To start, bring the water to a boil in a saucepan. Add the black tea bags, peaches, ginger, and honey, and let them steep for about 5 minutes. Remove the pan from heat and let it cool completely. Strain the mixture through a fine-mesh strainer into a pitcher. Refrigerate until chilled. Serve over ice with peach slices and fresh ginger slices for garnish (if using).

Rosemary and Grapefruit Spritzer

Rosemary and grapefruit spritzer is a refreshing and citrusy drink that's perfect for a summer picnic. To make it, you'll need:

- 2 cups of fresh grapefruit juice
- 1/4 cup of fresh rosemary leaves
- 1/4 cup of honey
- 2 cups of sparkling water
- Ice cubes
- Grapefruit slices and fresh rosemary sprigs for garnish (optional)

To start, add the grapefruit juice, rosemary leaves, and honey to a blender. Blend until smooth. Strain the mixture through a fine-mesh strainer into a pitcher. Stir in the sparkling water until well combined. Refrigerate until chilled. Serve over ice with grapefruit slices and fresh rosemary sprigs for garnish (if using).

Basil Limeade

Basil limeade is a vibrant and tangy drink that combines the herbaceous flavor of basil with the zing of lime. To make it, you'll need:

- 1 cup of fresh lime juice

- 1/2 cup of honey
- 8 cups of water
- 1/2 cup of fresh basil leaves
- Ice cubes
- Lime slices and fresh basil leaves for garnish (optional)

To start, add the lime juice, honey, and water to a pitcher. Stir until the honey is dissolved. Add the fresh basil leaves and muddle them gently to release the flavors. Refrigerate the mixture for at least 1 hour to allow the flavors to infuse. Serve over ice with lime slices and fresh basil leaves for garnish (if using).

Cucumber and Mint Cooler

Cucumber and mint cooler is a refreshing and hydrating drink that's perfect for a hot summer day. To make it, you'll need:

- 2 cucumbers, peeled and sliced
- 1/2 cup of fresh mint leaves
- 1/4 cup of fresh lime juice
- 4 cups of water
- 1/4 cup of honey
- Ice cubes
- Cucumber slices and fresh mint sprigs for garnish (optional)

To start, add the cucumber slices, mint leaves, lime juice, water, and honey to a blender. Blend until smooth. Strain the mixture through a fine-mesh strainer into a pitcher. Refrigerate until chilled. Serve over ice with cucumber slices and fresh mint sprigs for garnish (if using).

In conclusion, herb-infused iced beverages offer a refreshing and healthy way to quench your thirst during the summer months. From the soothing combination of lavender and lemon in lavender lemonade to the invigorating blend of mint and watermelon in the minty watermelon refresher, these recipes showcase the versatility of herbs in creating delicious and hydrating drinks. Whether you're hosting a backyard gathering or simply relaxing by the pool, these herb-infused iced beverages will elevate your refreshment game while providing a burst of flavor and a dose of health benefits. So, gather your herbs, mix up a pitcher of your favorite herb-infused iced beverage, and enjoy the cool and revitalizing flavors all summer long. Cheers to flavor and refreshment!

45. Herb-infused Energy Drinks

Herbs have been used for centuries in cooking and medicine due to their flavor and health benefits. Recently, herbs have been gaining popularity as an ingredient in energy drinks. Herb-infused energy drinks provide a natural boost of energy and offer numerous health benefits. In this chapter, we will explore the benefits of herb-infused energy drinks and provide recipes for you to try at home.

Benefits of Herb-Infused Energy Drinks

Boost Energy Levels: One of the primary benefits of herb-infused energy drinks is that they provide a natural boost of energy. Unlike traditional energy drinks that are often loaded with caffeine and sugar, herb-infused energy drinks use natural herbs to provide energy. Herbs such as ginseng and maca root have been shown to increase energy levels and reduce fatigue.

Improve Focus and Mental Clarity: Many herbs used in energy drinks have cognitive-enhancing properties that can improve focus and mental clarity. For example, ginkgo biloba is an herb that has been shown to improve memory and cognitive function.

Reduce Inflammation: Inflammation is a common cause of fatigue and can lead to a decrease in energy levels. Many herbs used in energy drinks have anti-inflammatory properties that can reduce inflammation and improve energy levels. Herbs such as turmeric and ginger have been shown to reduce inflammation in the body.

Provide Antioxidants: Many herbs used in energy drinks are rich in antioxidants, which can protect the body against free radicals. Free radicals can damage cells and lead to fatigue and decreased energy levels. Herbs such as green tea and rooibos are high in antioxidants and can provide numerous health benefits.

Improve Digestion: Digestive issues can lead to fatigue and decreased energy levels. Many herbs used in energy drinks have digestive-enhancing properties that can improve digestion and increase energy levels. Herbs such as peppermint and fennel can improve digestion and provide relief from digestive issues.

Recipes for Herb-Infused Energy Drinks

Lemon and Ginger Energy Drink

Ingredients:

- 1 lemon, juiced
- inch piece of ginger, peeled and grated
- 1 tablespoon honey
- 2 cups water
- Ice

Instructions:

In a large pitcher, combine the lemon juice, grated ginger, honey, and water.
Stir well to combine.
Add ice to the pitcher and stir.
Serve and enjoy!

Matcha Green Tea Energy Drink

Ingredients:

- 1 teaspoon matcha green tea powder
- 1 tablespoon honey
- 2 cups water
- Ice

Instructions:

In a large pitcher, combine the matcha green tea powder, honey, and water.
Stir well to combine.
Add ice to the pitcher and stir.
Serve and enjoy!

Mint and Cucumber Energy Drink

Ingredients:

- 1 cucumber, sliced
- 1/2 cup fresh mint leaves
- 2 cups water
- Ice

Instructions:

In a large pitcher, combine the cucumber slices, fresh mint leaves, and water.
Stir well to combine.
Add ice to the pitcher and stir.
Serve and enjoy!

Hibiscus and Orange Energy Drink

Ingredients:

- 1/4 cup dried hibiscus flowers
- 1 orange, juiced
- 2 cups water
- Ice

Instructions:

In a large pitcher, combine the dried hibiscus flowers, orange juice, and water. Stir well to combine.

Add ice to the pitcher and stir.

Serve and enjoy!

In conclusion, herb-infused energy drinks provide a natural and healthy way to boost energy levels and improve overall health. By using natural herbs instead of artificial ingredients, herb-infused energy drinks offer numerous health benefits without the negative side effects commonly associated with traditional energy drinks. Whether you're looking to improve focus and mental clarity, reduce inflammation, or simply boost your energy levels, there's an herb-infused energy drink recipe for you to try.

By experimenting with different herbs and flavors, you can create your own unique energy drinks that are tailored to your personal tastes and needs. Not only will you be able to enjoy the natural energy boost and health benefits of herb-infused energy drinks, but you'll also be able to impress your friends and family with your culinary skills.

Incorporating herbs into your diet is a simple and effective way to add flavor and health to your meals and drinks. Whether you're cooking with herbs or making herb-infused energy drinks, there's no shortage of ways to incorporate these powerful plants into your daily routine. So why not give herb-infused energy drinks a try and see for yourself the amazing benefits they have to offer?

46. Herb-infused Protein Shakes

Protein shakes have been a staple in the fitness and health community for decades. They are a convenient and easy way to fuel your body with the nutrients it needs to build and repair muscle tissue. However, many protein shakes are lacking in flavor and can become boring after a while. Herb-infused protein shakes are a great way to add flavor and health benefits to your daily routine. In this chapter, we will explore the benefits of herb-infused protein shakes and provide recipes for you to try at home.

Benefits of Herb-Infused Protein Shakes

Improve Digestion: Digestive issues can hinder your body's ability to absorb nutrients, including protein. Many herbs used in protein shakes have digestive-enhancing properties that can improve digestion and increase your body's ability to absorb protein. Herbs such as ginger and mint can improve digestion and provide relief from digestive issues.

Boost Immune System: A strong immune system is essential for overall health and can be especially important for athletes and fitness enthusiasts. Many herbs used in protein shakes are high in antioxidants and can help boost the immune system. Herbs such as turmeric and cinnamon have been shown to have anti-inflammatory and immune-boosting properties.

Provide Antioxidants: Antioxidants are important for protecting the body against free radicals. Free radicals can cause oxidative stress and damage to cells, which can lead to inflammation and disease. Many herbs used in protein shakes are high in antioxidants, including green tea and matcha.

Reduce Inflammation: Inflammation is a common cause of muscle soreness and can lead to decreased performance in the gym. Many herbs used in protein shakes have anti-inflammatory properties that can reduce inflammation and improve muscle recovery. Herbs such as ginger and turmeric have been shown to reduce inflammation in the body.

Add Flavor: Let's face it, protein shakes can be boring and bland. Adding herbs to your protein shakes is a great way to add flavor and variety to your diet. Herbs such as basil and mint can provide a refreshing and unique taste to your shakes.

Recipes for Herb-Infused Protein Shakes

Ginger and Pineapple Protein Shake

Ingredients:

- 1 scoop vanilla protein powder
- 1 cup unsweetened almond milk
- 1/2 cup frozen pineapple chunks
- 1 tablespoon grated ginger
- 1 teaspoon honey
- Handful of ice

Instructions:

Add all ingredients to a blender and blend until smooth. Pour into a glass and enjoy!

Matcha Green Tea Protein Shake

Ingredients:

- 1 scoop vanilla protein powder
- 1 cup unsweetened almond milk
- 1 teaspoon matcha green tea powder
- 1/2 banana
- 1 teaspoon honey
- Handful of ice

Instructions:

Add all ingredients to a blender and blend until smooth. Pour into a glass and enjoy!

Mint Chocolate Protein Shake

Ingredients:

- 1 scoop chocolate protein powder
- 1 cup unsweetened almond milk
- Handful of fresh mint leaves
- 1/2 banana
- Handful of ice

Instructions:

Add all ingredients to a blender and blend until smooth. Pour into a glass and enjoy!

Turmeric and Mango Protein Shake

Ingredients:

- 1 scoop vanilla protein powder

- 1 cup unsweetened almond milk
- 1/2 cup frozen mango chunks
- 1 teaspoon turmeric powder
- 1 teaspoon honey
- Handful of ice

Instructions:

Add all ingredients to a blender and blend until smooth.

Pour into a glass and enjoy!

In conclusion, herb-infused protein shakes are a great way to add flavor and health benefits to your daily routine. Herbs such as ginger, turmeric, and mint can improve digestion, boost the immune system, provide antioxidants, reduce inflammation, and add flavor to your shakes. With the recipes provided, you can easily create your own herb-infused protein shakes at home and enjoy the benefits of these powerful herbs. Incorporating herbs into your diet is a simple and effective way to add flavor and health to your meals and drinks, so why not give herb-infused protein shakes a try and see for yourself the amazing benefits they have to offer?

47. Making the Perfect Herb-infused Ice Cream

Ice cream is a beloved dessert that is enjoyed by people all around the world. Adding herbs to ice cream is a great way to infuse it with unique and delicious flavors while also providing health benefits. In this chapter, we will explore the art of making the perfect herb-infused ice cream and provide recipes for you to try at home.

Benefits of Herb-infused Ice Cream

Digestive Health: Many herbs used in ice cream have digestive-enhancing properties that can improve digestion and provide relief from digestive issues. For example, mint has been used for centuries as a natural digestive aid.

Anti-inflammatory Properties: Inflammation is a common cause of many health problems, including heart disease, diabetes, and cancer. Many herbs used in ice cream have anti-inflammatory properties, which can help to reduce inflammation in the body. For example, ginger has been shown to reduce inflammation and improve heart health.

Antioxidant Benefits: Herbs are known for their antioxidant properties, which can help to protect the body against free radical damage. For example, lavender has been shown to have antioxidant properties that can help to protect against oxidative stress.

Flavor Enhancement: Adding herbs to ice cream is a great way to infuse it with unique and delicious flavors. Herbs such as basil, rosemary, and thyme can add a savory twist to ice cream, while lavender and chamomile can add a sweet and floral note.

Tips for Making the Perfect Herb-infused Ice Cream

Use Fresh Herbs: When making herb-infused ice cream, it is important to use fresh herbs rather than dried ones. Fresh herbs have a more potent flavor and aroma, which will help to infuse the ice cream with more flavor.

Steep the Herbs: To infuse the ice cream with the flavor of the herbs, it is important to steep them in the cream or milk before making the ice cream. Steeping the herbs will help to extract their essential oils, which will infuse the ice cream with their flavor and aroma.

Strain the Mixture: After steeping the herbs, it is important to strain the mixture to remove any pieces of herb that may be left behind. This will ensure that the ice cream has a smooth texture and does not have any pieces of herb in it.

Chill the Mixture: Before making the ice cream, it is important to chill the mixture in the refrigerator. This will help to ensure that the ice cream freezes properly and has a smooth texture.

Recipes for Herb-infused Ice Cream

Basil Ice Cream

Ingredients:

- 2 cups heavy cream
- 1 cup whole milk
- 1 cup fresh basil leaves
- 3/4 cup granulated sugar
- 6 egg yolks
- Pinch of salt

Instructions:

In a medium saucepan, combine the cream, milk, and basil leaves. Heat the mixture over medium heat until it begins to steam, then remove from heat and let steep for 30 minutes.

In a separate bowl, whisk together the sugar and egg yolks until pale and thick.

Reheat the cream mixture until it begins to steam again. Slowly pour the hot cream mixture into the egg mixture, whisking constantly.

Pour the mixture back into the saucepan and cook over medium heat, stirring constantly, until the mixture thickens and coats the back of a spoon.

Strain the mixture through a fine-mesh sieve into a bowl, and stir in a pinch of salt.

Chill the mixture in the refrigerator for at least 4 hours or overnight.

Pour the chilled mixture into an ice cream maker and churn according to the manufacturer's instructions.

Transfer the ice cream to a container and freeze until firm, about 4 hours.

Lavender Honey Ice Cream

Ingredients:

- 2 cups heavy cream
- 1 cup whole milk
- 1/2 cup dried lavender flowers
- 3/4 cup honey

- 6 egg yolks
- Pinch of salt

Instructions:

In a medium saucepan, combine the cream, milk, and lavender flowers. Heat the mixture over medium heat until it begins to steam, then remove from heat and let steep for 30 minutes.

In a separate bowl, whisk together the honey and egg yolks until pale and thick.

Reheat the cream mixture until it begins to steam again. Slowly pour the hot cream mixture into the egg mixture, whisking constantly.

Pour the mixture back into the saucepan and cook over medium heat, stirring constantly, until the mixture thickens and coats the back of a spoon.

Strain the mixture through a fine-mesh sieve into a bowl, and stir in a pinch of salt.

Chill the mixture in the refrigerator for at least 4 hours or overnight.

Pour the chilled mixture into an ice cream maker and churn according to the manufacturer's instructions.

Transfer the ice cream to a container and freeze until firm, about 4 hours.

Ginger Turmeric Ice Cream

Ingredients:

- 2 cups heavy cream
- 1 cup whole milk
- 2-inch piece of fresh ginger, peeled and thinly sliced
- 1 tablespoon ground turmeric
- 3/4 cup granulated sugar
- 6 egg yolks
- Pinch of salt

Instructions:

In a medium saucepan, combine the cream, milk, ginger, and turmeric. Heat the mixture over medium heat until it begins to steam, then remove from heat and let steep for 30 minutes.

In a separate bowl, whisk together the sugar and egg yolks until pale and thick.

Reheat the cream mixture until it begins to steam again. Slowly pour the hot cream mixture into the egg mixture, whisking constantly.

Pour the mixture back into the saucepan and cook over medium heat, stirring constantly, until the mixture thickens and coats the back of a spoon.

Strain the mixture through a fine-mesh sieve into a bowl, and stir in a pinch of salt.
Chill the mixture in the refrigerator for at least 4 hours or overnight.
Pour the chilled mixture into an ice cream maker and churn according to the manufacturer's instructions.
Transfer the ice cream to a container and freeze until firm, about 4 hours.
In conclusion, herb-infused ice cream is a delicious and healthy alternative to traditional ice cream. With the recipes provided, you can easily make your own herb-infused ice cream at home and enjoy the amazing flavor and health benefits of herbs. Remember to use fresh herbs, steep them properly, strain the mixture, and chill it before making the ice cream. Give these recipes a try and let your taste buds and health benefit from the wonderful world of herb-infused ice cream.

48. Herb-infused Sorbet and Granita Recipes

When it comes to cool and refreshing desserts, sorbet and granita are among the most popular choices. Both are icy treats that can be enjoyed on a hot summer day, but the difference lies in the texture. Sorbet is smooth and velvety, while granita has a more granular texture. With the addition of herbs, these desserts become even more flavorful and healthy. In this chapter, we'll explore some delicious herb-infused sorbet and granita recipes that will tantalize your taste buds and offer a variety of health benefits.

Mint Lime Sorbet

Ingredients:

- 1 cup water
- 1 cup granulated sugar
- 1 cup fresh mint leaves
- 1/2 cup fresh lime juice
- 1 tablespoon lime zest
- Pinch of salt

Instructions:

In a medium saucepan, combine the water, sugar, and mint leaves. Bring the mixture to a boil, stirring until the sugar dissolves.

Remove from heat and let the mixture steep for 30 minutes.

Strain the mixture through a fine-mesh sieve into a bowl.

Stir in the lime juice, lime zest, and a pinch of salt.

Chill the mixture in the refrigerator for at least 4 hours or overnight.

Pour the chilled mixture into an ice cream maker and churn according to the manufacturer's instructions.

Transfer the sorbet to a container and freeze until firm, about 4 hours.

Lavender Lemon Sorbet

Ingredients:

- 1 cup water
- 1 cup granulated sugar
- 1/2 cup fresh lavender flowers
- 1/2 cup fresh lemon juice
- 1 tablespoon lemon zest

- Pinch of salt

Instructions:

In a medium saucepan, combine the water, sugar, and lavender flowers. Bring the mixture to a boil, stirring until the sugar dissolves.

Remove from heat and let the mixture steep for 30 minutes.

Strain the mixture through a fine-mesh sieve into a bowl.

Stir in the lemon juice, lemon zest, and a pinch of salt.

Chill the mixture in the refrigerator for at least 4 hours or overnight.

Pour the chilled mixture into an ice cream maker and churn according to the manufacturer's instructions.

Transfer the sorbet to a container and freeze until firm, about 4 hours.

Pineapple Basil Granita

Ingredients:

- 1 cup water
- 1 cup granulated sugar
- 1/2 cup fresh basil leaves
- 1 small ripe pineapple, peeled, cored, and chopped
- Juice of 1 lime
- Pinch of salt

Instructions:

In a medium saucepan, combine the water, sugar, and basil leaves. Bring the mixture to a boil, stirring until the sugar dissolves.

Remove from heat and let the mixture steep for 30 minutes.

Strain the mixture through a fine-mesh sieve into a blender.

Add the chopped pineapple, lime juice, and a pinch of salt to the blender.

Blend until smooth.

Pour the mixture into a shallow, freezer-safe container and freeze for 1 hour.

After 1 hour, use a fork to scrape the frozen mixture into small, granular pieces.

Freeze for another 3 hours, scraping with a fork every hour to create a granular texture.

Rosemary Grapefruit Granita

Ingredients:

- 1 cup water
- 1 cup granulated sugar
- 2 sprigs fresh rosemary

- 1 cup fresh grapefruit juice
- 1 tablespoon grapefruit zest
- Pinch of salt

Instructions:

In a medium saucepan, combine the water, sugar, and rosemary sprigs. Bring the mixture to a boil, stirring until the sugar dissolves.

Remove from heat and let the mixture steep for 30 minutes.

Strain the mixture through a fine-mesh sieve into a bowl.

Stir in the grapefruit juice, grapefruit zest, and a pinch of salt.

Pour the mixture into a shallow, freezer-safe container and freeze for 1 hour.

After 1 hour, use a fork to scrape the frozen mixture into small, granular pieces.

Freeze for another 3 hours, scraping with a fork every hour to create a granular texture.

Basil Watermelon Granita

Ingredients:

- 1 cup water
- 1 cup granulated sugar
- 1/2 cup fresh basil leaves
- 4 cups seedless watermelon, cubed
- Juice of 1 lime
- Pinch of salt

Instructions:

In a medium saucepan, combine the water, sugar, and basil leaves. Bring the mixture to a boil, stirring until the sugar dissolves.

Remove from heat and let the mixture steep for 30 minutes.

Strain the mixture through a fine-mesh sieve into a blender.

Add the watermelon, lime juice, and a pinch of salt to the blender.

Blend until smooth.

Pour the mixture into a shallow, freezer-safe container and freeze for 1 hour.

After 1 hour, use a fork to scrape the frozen mixture into small, granular pieces.

Freeze for another 3 hours, scraping with a fork every hour to create a granular texture.

In conclusion, herb-infused sorbet and granita recipes offer a refreshing and healthy way to enjoy the benefits of herbs. The recipes shared in this chapter are easy to make and packed with flavor. Whether you're in the mood for something sweet or tangy, these icy treats will satisfy your cravings while providing a variety of health benefits. From the cooling effect of mint to the calming properties of lavender, the herbs in these recipes offer a range of health benefits that are worth exploring. So, the next time you're in the mood for a cool and refreshing dessert, try one of these herb-infused sorbet or granita recipes and enjoy the delicious taste and health benefits!

49. Herb-infused Yogurt and Cheese Recipes

Yogurt and cheese are staples in many people's diets, and for good reason. They are a great source of protein, calcium, and other essential nutrients. However, they can also be a bit bland on their own. Fortunately, adding herbs to yogurt and cheese can not only add flavor but also provide additional health benefits. In this chapter, we will explore a variety of herb-infused yogurt and cheese recipes that are not only delicious but also nutritious.

Herbed Yogurt Dip

Ingredients:

- 1 cup plain Greek yogurt
- 1/4 cup chopped fresh herbs (such as dill, parsley, chives, or cilantro)
- 2 cloves garlic, minced
- 1 tablespoon lemon juice
- 1/4 teaspoon salt
- Pinch of black pepper

Instructions:

In a medium bowl, combine the Greek yogurt, herbs, garlic, lemon juice, salt, and black pepper.

Mix until well combined.

Cover and refrigerate for at least 30 minutes to allow the flavors to meld.

Serve with vegetables or pita chips.

Herbed Goat Cheese Spread

Ingredients:

- 4 oz. goat cheese, softened
- 1 tablespoon chopped fresh herbs (such as rosemary, thyme, or basil)
- 1 tablespoon olive oil
- 1/4 teaspoon salt
- Pinch of black pepper

Instructions:

In a small bowl, combine the goat cheese, herbs, olive oil, salt, and black pepper.

Mix until well combined.

Spread on crackers or toasted bread.

Herbed Ricotta Dip

Ingredients:

- 1 cup ricotta cheese
- 1/4 cup chopped fresh herbs (such as basil, oregano, or parsley)
- 1/4 teaspoon garlic powder
- 1/4 teaspoon salt
- Pinch of black pepper

Instructions:

In a medium bowl, combine the ricotta cheese, herbs, garlic powder, salt, and black pepper.

Mix until well combined.

Cover and refrigerate for at least 30 minutes to allow the flavors to meld.

Serve with crackers or vegetables.

Herbed Feta Cheese

Ingredients:

- 4 oz. feta cheese, crumbled
- 1 tablespoon chopped fresh herbs (such as mint, dill, or parsley)
- 1 tablespoon olive oil
- 1/4 teaspoon black pepper

Instructions:

In a small bowl, combine the feta cheese, herbs, olive oil, and black pepper.

Mix until well combined.

Serve on a salad or with crackers.

Herbed Cottage Cheese

Ingredients:

- 1 cup cottage cheese
- 1/4 cup chopped fresh herbs (such as chives, parsley, or dill)
- 1/4 teaspoon garlic powder
- 1/4 teaspoon salt
- Pinch of black pepper

Instructions:

In a medium bowl, combine the cottage cheese, herbs, garlic powder, salt, and black pepper.

Mix until well combined.

Cover and refrigerate for at least 30 minutes to allow the flavors to meld.

Serve as a side dish or with crackers.

In conclusion, herb-infused yogurt and cheese recipes are a simple and tasty way to elevate your dishes while also providing added health benefits. With a variety of fresh herbs to choose from, you can customize your yogurt and cheese recipes to your liking. Whether you prefer the tanginess of goat cheese or the creaminess of ricotta, adding herbs can take your dish to the next level. These recipes can be used as dips, spreads, or toppings for salads and other dishes, making them versatile additions to any meal. So go ahead and experiment with different herb combinations and discover the endless possibilities of herb-infused yogurt and cheese recipes.

50. Creating a Herb-infused Spice Blend for Any Dish

Spices are an essential part of cooking. They add flavor, aroma, and color to dishes, transforming a bland meal into a delicious culinary experience. However, many store-bought spice blends are loaded with salt, sugar, and other unhealthy additives. Creating your own herb-infused spice blend not only allows you to control the ingredients, but also provides the added health benefits of using fresh herbs. In this chapter, we will explore the benefits of herb-infused spice blends and provide a simple recipe for creating your own blend at home.

Benefits of Herb-infused Spice Blends

Herb-infused spice blends offer numerous health benefits that go beyond just adding flavor to dishes. Herbs such as thyme, oregano, and rosemary contain antioxidants and anti-inflammatory compounds that can help boost the immune system and reduce the risk of chronic diseases. By using fresh herbs in your spice blend, you are incorporating these beneficial compounds into your cooking.

Another benefit of creating your own spice blend is the ability to control the amount of salt and sugar used. Many store-bought spice blends are high in sodium, which can lead to high blood pressure and other health issues. By making your own blend, you can adjust the salt content to your liking or even eliminate it altogether. Similarly, by avoiding added sugar, you can reduce your overall sugar intake and improve your health.

Creating Your Own Herb-infused Spice Blend

Creating your own herb-infused spice blend is a simple process that allows you to customize the flavor to your liking. Below is a basic recipe for creating a versatile spice blend that can be used in a variety of dishes.

Ingredients:

- 2 tbsp dried oregano
- 2 tbsp dried thyme
- 2 tbsp dried rosemary
- 2 tbsp dried basil
- 2 tbsp garlic powder

- 1 tbsp onion powder
- 1 tsp black pepper

Instructions:

In a small bowl, combine all the ingredients.

Mix well to ensure the herbs and spices are evenly distributed.

Store in an airtight container in a cool, dry place.

This basic recipe can be modified to suit your taste preferences or the dish you are preparing. For example, if you want to add some heat, you can include a teaspoon of red pepper flakes. If you prefer a sweeter flavor, you can add a teaspoon of cinnamon or nutmeg.

Using Your Herb-infused Spice Blend

Once you have created your own herb-infused spice blend, the possibilities for using it are endless. Here are some ideas for incorporating your blend into various dishes:

Roasted Vegetables: Toss vegetables such as carrots, broccoli, and cauliflower with olive oil and a tablespoon of your spice blend before roasting for added flavor.

Grilled Meat: Rub your spice blend onto chicken, beef, or pork before grilling for a flavorful and aromatic result.

Soups and Stews: Add a tablespoon of your spice blend to soups and stews for a depth of flavor that will make your dish stand out.

Pasta Dishes: Use your spice blend to season tomato sauce for pasta dishes or sprinkle it over cooked pasta for added flavor.

Dips and Spreads: Mix your spice blend with yogurt or sour cream for a delicious dip or spread for vegetables or crackers.

In conclusion, creating your own herb-infused spice blend is a great way to add flavor and health benefits to any dish. By using fresh herbs, you are incorporating beneficial compounds into your cooking, while also having the ability to control the amount of salt and sugar used. With endless possibilities for use, your herb-infused spice blend can become a staple in your kitchen, elevating the flavor of your meals and contributing to your overall health and wellbeing. So go ahead and experiment with different herbs and spices to create a blend that is perfect for your taste preferences and dietary needs.

Epilogue

As we come to the end of "Cooking with Herbs: Adding Flavor and Health," we hope that this book has inspired you to explore the world of herbs and all the delicious and healthful possibilities they offer. Herbs have been used for thousands of years for their culinary and medicinal properties, and their popularity continues to grow in the modern age.

In this book, we have explored a wide range of herbs and how to use them in your cooking. From simple dishes to more complex recipes, we have shown how herbs can elevate the flavors of your meals and add a range of health benefits. By using fresh herbs in your cooking, you are not only adding flavor but also incorporating important vitamins, minerals, and antioxidants into your diet.

One of the key takeaways from this book is that cooking with herbs doesn't have to be complicated or time-consuming. With a little bit of knowledge and some experimentation, you can easily incorporate herbs into your everyday cooking. Whether you are making a simple salad or a complex entree, adding herbs can take your dish to the next level and make it a memorable experience for yourself and your guests.

We also hope that this book has inspired you to grow your own herbs. Fresh herbs are readily available in most grocery stores, but growing your own herbs can be a fun and rewarding experience. Not only does it provide you with fresh herbs on demand, but it also adds an element of sustainability to your cooking.

Finally, we want to emphasize the importance of health and wellness. The herbs we have discussed in this book offer numerous health benefits, including anti-inflammatory, antioxidant, and antimicrobial properties. Incorporating these herbs into your diet can help you maintain good health and prevent chronic diseases. We hope that this book has been informative, inspiring, and enjoyable. Our goal was to provide you with a comprehensive guide to using herbs in your cooking, and we believe that we have accomplished that goal. We hope that you continue to explore the world of herbs and all the delicious and healthful possibilities they offer. Happy cooking!

*****

Milton Keynes UK
Ingram Content Group UK Ltd.
UKHW041827161023
430722UK00001B/129

9 798223 063179